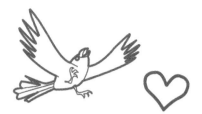

stop Making Art and Die

Rich Théroux

UpRoute
Bright Books with Bite

An Imprint of Durvile Publications Ltd.

UpRoute
Bright Books with Bite

UpRoute Books and Media
An Imprint of Durvile Publications Ltd.
Calgary, Alberta, Canada

Copyright © 2016 by Rich Théroux

National Library of Canada
Cataloguing in Publications Data
Written and Illustrated by: Théroux, Rich
Stop Making Art and Die: Survival Activities for Artists
Information on this title www.durvile.com and www.uproute.ca
ISBN 978-0-9947352-2-5 (print pbk), | ISBN 978-0-9952322-3-5 (epub)

1. Art | 2. Art Techniques | 3. Biography
Book One in the 'Artist Survival Activities' Series
First edition | First printing 2016
Editor: Lorene Shyba

Printed in Canada

Durvile Publications Ltd. is a member of Book Publishers Association of Alberta (BPAA).
We would like to acknowledge the support of the Alberta Government through the Alberta Media Fund.

for Oliver G. Sparkes, Enriquito,
and you
　　　orphans

Another book by Rich Théroux

We Kicked a Hole in the Sky
an analogue catalogue of 198 poems
Compiled by Jess Szabo
Rumble House: 2016

Survival Activities

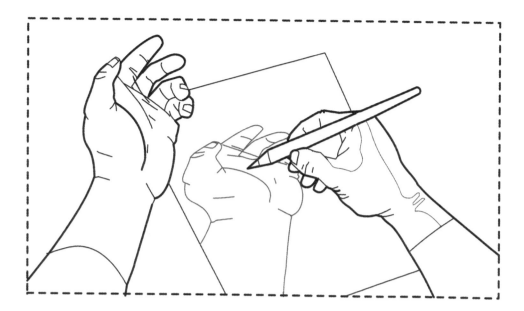

This is the story of how the GORILLA House became the RUMBLE House. It's a story of more than five thousand people, some of whom are in this book. Whenever possible I use real people and real stories. And though it's not exclusively my story, it's the story as I saw it. For that I apologize if it seems like I've drawn my own hands more often than yours. The common theme is that I was in the room and I never needed to ask permission to tell the story with or by using these hands.

There's room for you below to draw your own hands.
One will be easier than the other.

Try out the space at the back of the book to stretch out and draw your hands life sized.

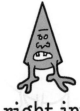 be fearless
colour, draw, and doodle
right into this book

feel free to
colour outside
of the lines any time

stop making art and die

Here is a warmup! Make art or die.

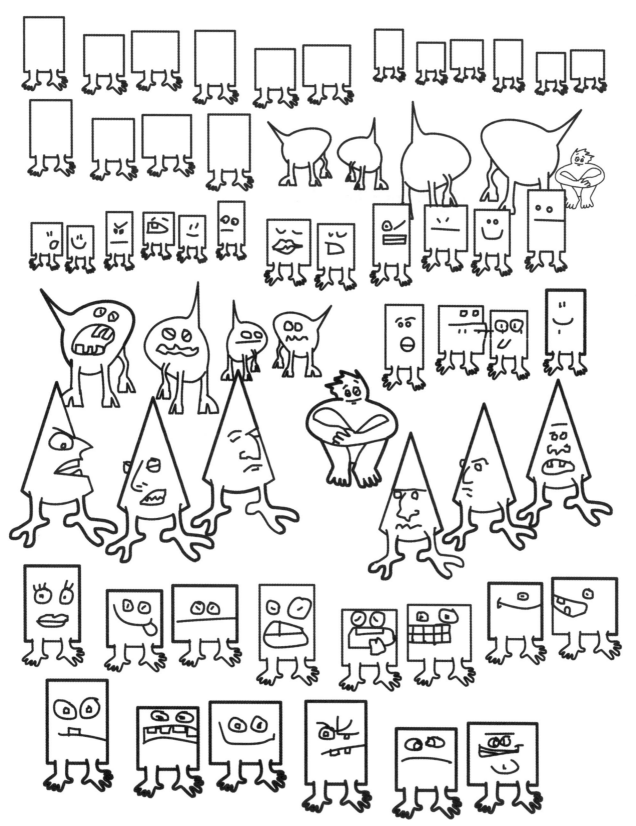

No one

said

this

would

be

easy

SURVIVAL ACTIVITY I

Search
for
meaning

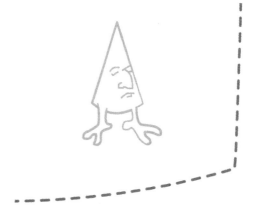

The Owner(ous)

This *moment is precious, dig deep*

Place *your heart on the table and ask yourself*

Is *this thing still alive? Choose your most*

Sacred *weapon, maybe a pencil, maybe a pen, maybe a brush*

Do *not ignore this naked beast, it beats*

Not *just from habit, it beats courageously for you*

Take *note of the whole experience of separation*

It *is not essential to soak in this loneliness*

For *as long as you can bathe in it, take for*

Granted *this enriched moment, this precious second*

It *won't fester under your attentive gaze, remember your*

Will *is infinite, remember you are not alone...*

Not *here anyway! You are safe at*

Last*, we can communicate with the others*

Forever *is a long time to have waited for this*

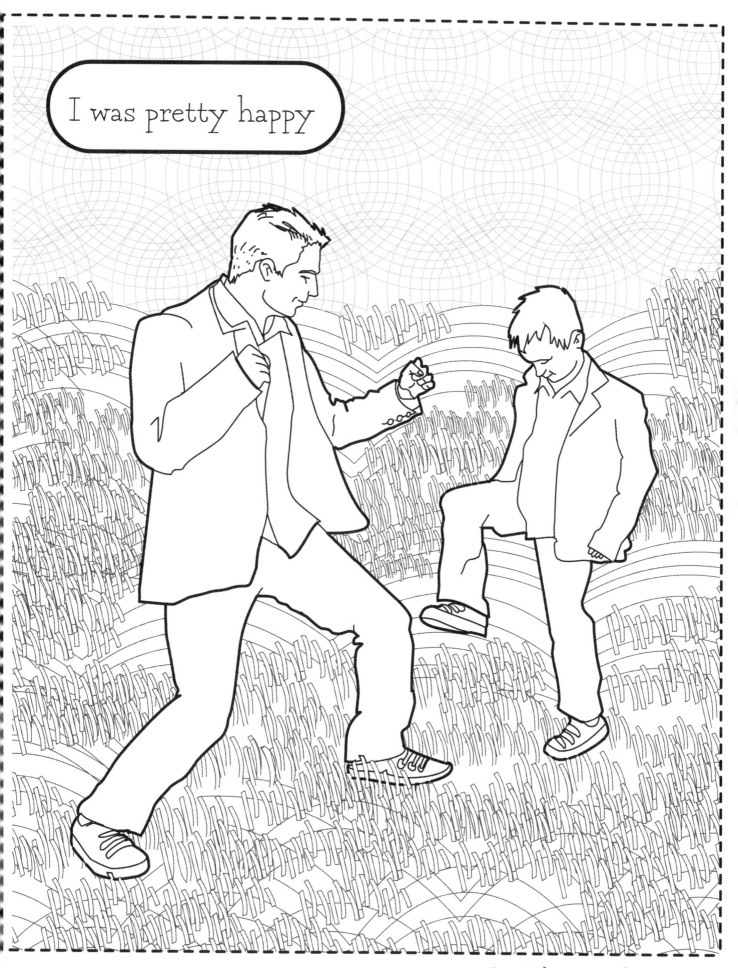

What are 50 things that make you happy?

1. _ _ _ _ _ _ _ _ _ _
2. _ _ _ _ _ _ _ _ _ _
3. _ _ _ _ _ _ _ _ _ _
4. _ _ _ _ _ _ _ _ _ _
5. _ _ _ _ _ _ _ _ _ _
6. _ _ _ _ _ _ _ _ _ _
7. _ _ _ _ _ _ _ _ _ _
8. _ _ _ _ _ _ _ _ _ _
9. _ _ _ _ _ _ _ _ _ _
10. _ _ _ _ _ _ _ _ _ _
11. _ _ _ _ _ _ _ _ _ _
12. _ _ _ _ _ _ _ _ _ _
13. _ _ _ _ _ _ _ _ _ _
14. _ _ _ _ _ _ _ _ _ _
15. _ _ _ _ _ _ _ _ _ _
16. _ _ _ _ _ _ _ _ _ _
17. _ _ _ _ _ _ _ _ _ _
18. _ _ _ _ _ _ _ _ _ _
19. _ _ _ _ _ _ _ _ _ _
20. _ _ _ _ _ _ _ _ _ _

21. _ _ _ _ _ _ _ _ _ _
22. _ _ _ _ _ _ _ _ _ _
23. _ _ _ _ _ _ _ _ _ _
24. _ _ _ _ _ _ _ _ _ _
25. _ _ _ _ _ _ _ _ _ _
26. _ _ _ _ _ _ _ _ _ _
27. _ _ _ _ _ _ _ _ _ _
28. _ _ _ _ _ _ _ _ _ _
29. _ _ _ _ _ _ _ _ _ _
30. _ _ _ _ _ _ _ _ _ _
31. _ _ _ _ _ _ _ _ _ _
32. _ _ _ _ _ _ _ _ _ _
33. _ _ _ _ _ _ _ _ _ _
34. _ _ _ _ _ _ _ _ _ _
35. _ _ _ _ _ _ _ _ _ _
36. _ _ _ _ _ _ _ _ _ _
37. _ _ _ _ _ _ _ _ _ _
38. _ _ _ _ _ _ _ _ _ _
39. _ _ _ _ _ _ _ _ _ _
40. _ _ _ _ _ _ _ _ _ _

41. _ _ _ _ _ _ _ _ _ _
42. _ _ _ _ _ _ _ _ _ _
43. _ _ _ _ _ _ _ _ _ _
44. _ _ _ _ _ _ _ _ _ _
45. _ _ _ _ _ _ _ _ _ _
46. _ _ _ _ _ _ _ _ _ _
47. _ _ _ _ _ _ _ _ _ _
48. _ _ _ _ _ _ _ _ _ _
49. _ _ _ _ _ _ _ _ _ _
50. _ _ _ _ _ _ _ _ _ _

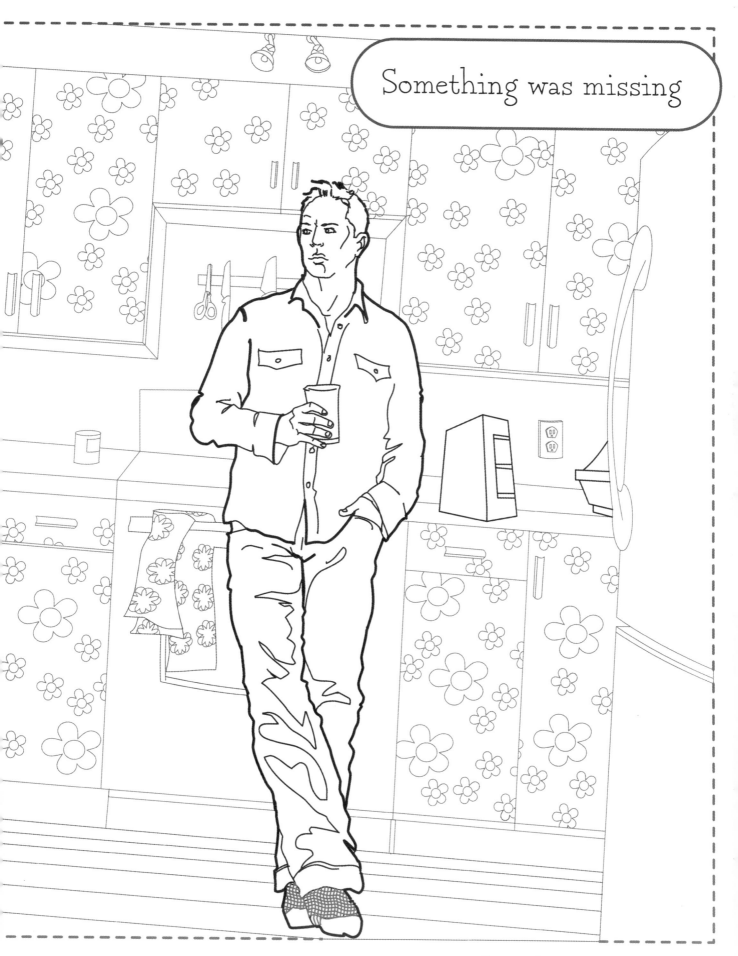

Something was missing

Can you think of five things that are missing from your life?

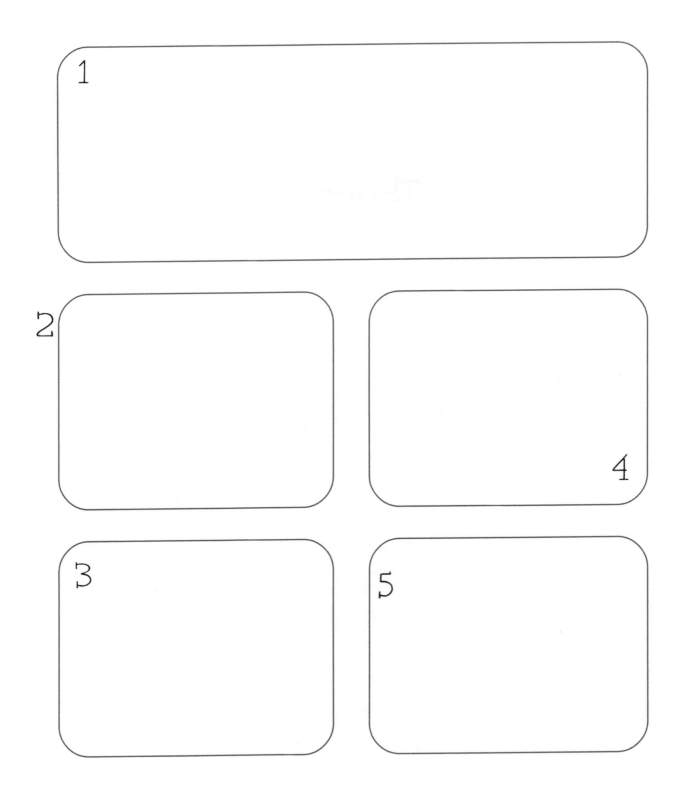

1

2

4

3

5

SURVIVAL ACTIVITY II

The urge
to
modify

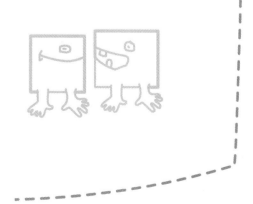

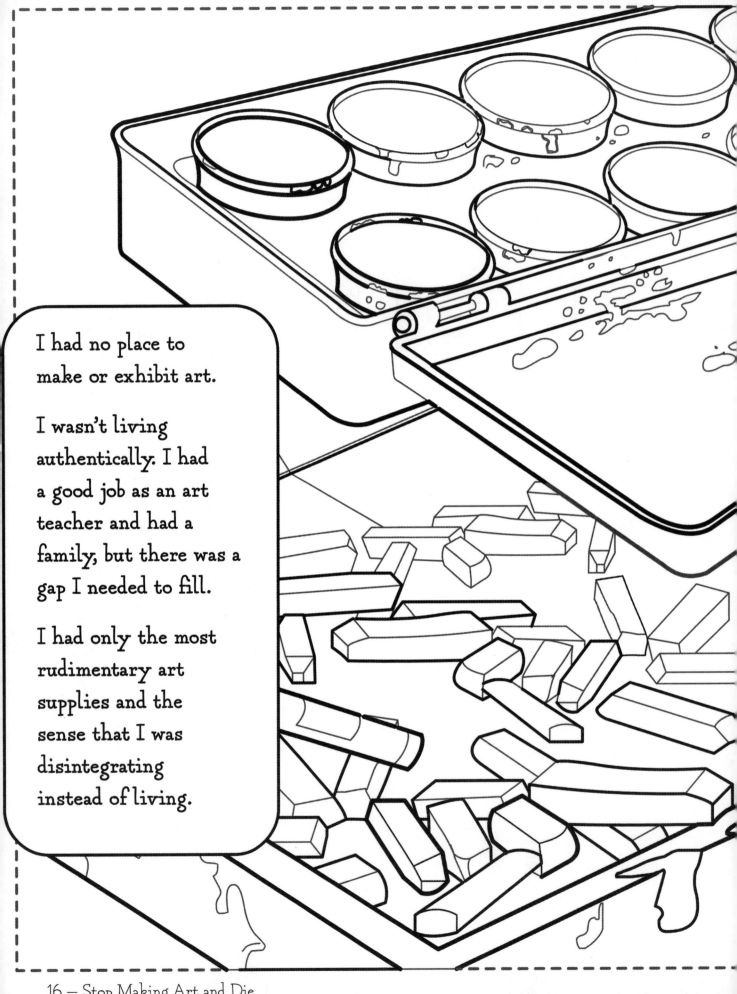

I had no place to make or exhibit art.

I wasn't living authentically. I had a good job as an art teacher and had a family, but there was a gap I needed to fill.

I had only the most rudimentary art supplies and the sense that I was disintegrating instead of living.

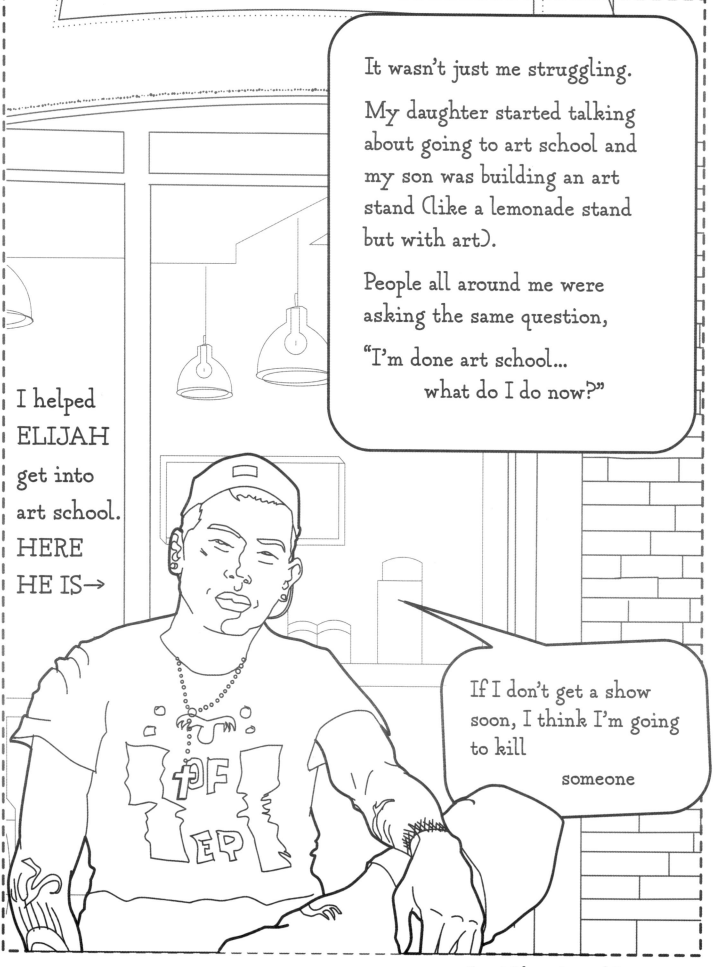

Let me run

dear god let me run

just once

without these boots

in the dark

by myself

without anyone

holding me back

dear god let me

run just once

let me show you what

these feet can do

while i still can

just once

Can
you
try
writing
your
own
poem
about
running
free?

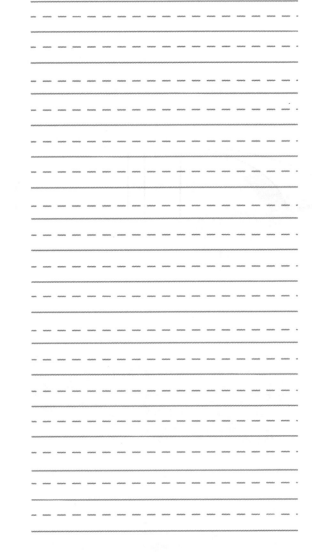

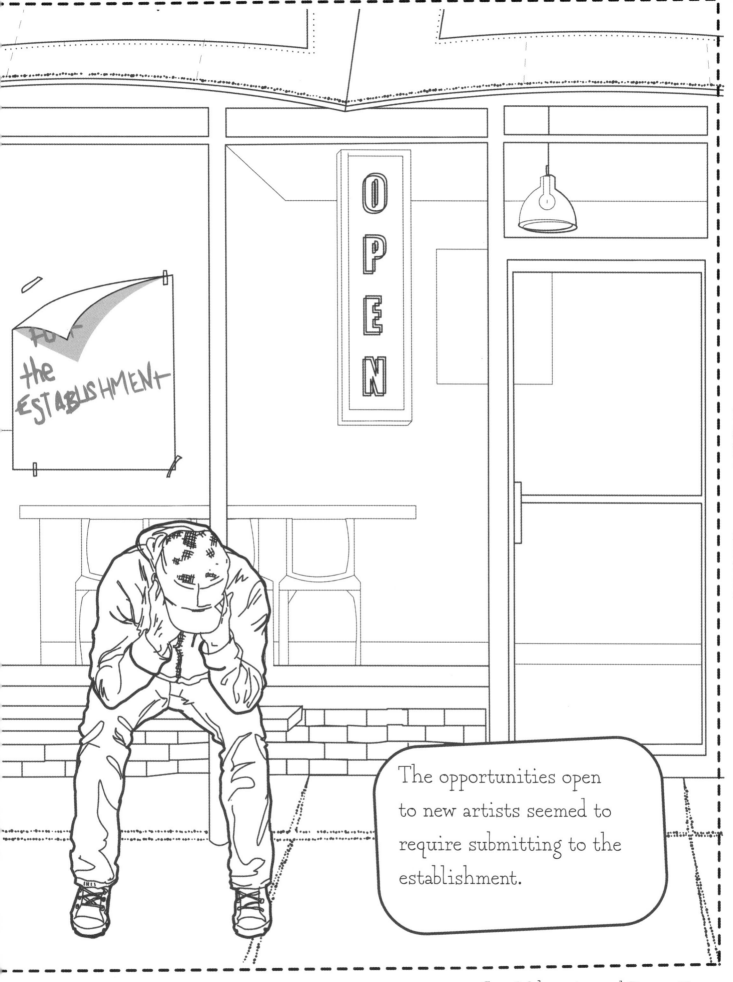

The opportunities open to new artists seemed to require submitting to the establishment.

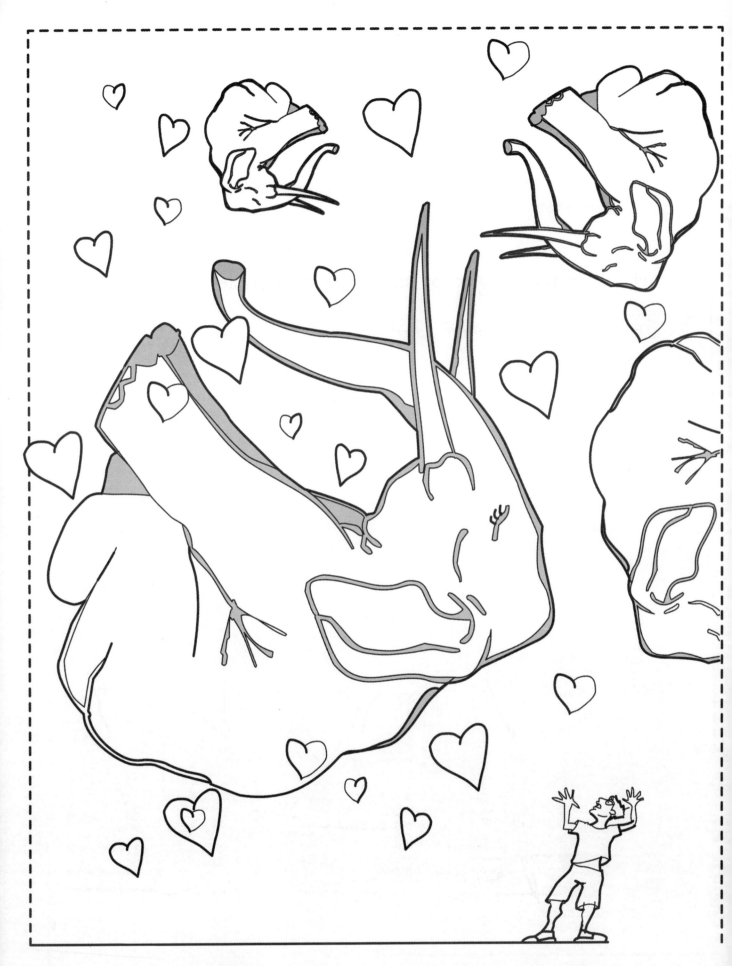

I sat down and started writing business plans.

I wrote a lot of plans. I thought, if a coffee shop can stay open, and if an art studio could stay open, and art galleries stay open, and places that run art classes stay open, then surely an Art-Studio/Gallery-Coffee shop, art lesson teaching co-op should be sustainable!

Or at least, I figured I wouldn't lose my house.

I was wrong about most of that stuff,
but I was right enough.

I did lose my house.

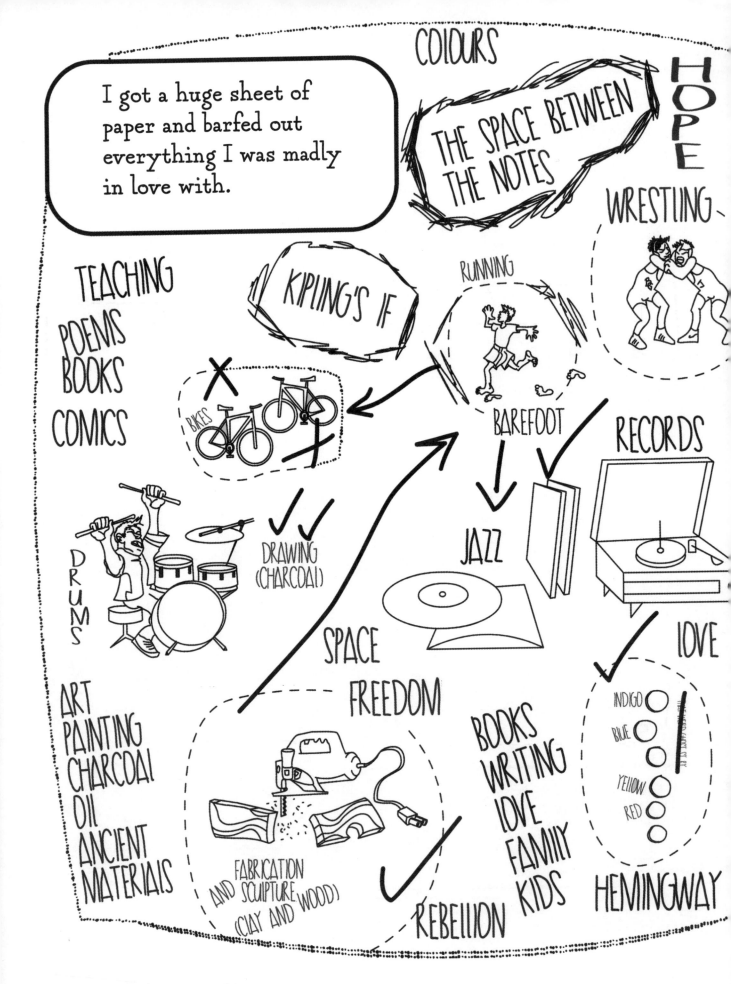

BARF UP THINGS YOU ARE MADLY IN LOVE WITH.

What artists really matter?

1. _ _ _ _ _ _ _ _ _ _ _ _ _
2. _ _ _ _ _ _ _ _ _ _ _ _ _
3. _ _ _ _ _ _ _ _ _ _ _ _ _
4. _ _ _ _ _ _ _ _ _ _ _ _ _
5. _ _ _ _ _ _ _ _ _ _ _ _ _

What can't you live without?

1. _ _ _ _ _ _ _ _ _ _ _ _ _
2. _ _ _ _ _ _ _ _ _ _ _ _ _
3. _ _ _ _ _ _ _ _ _ _ _ _ _
4. _ _ _ _ _ _ _ _ _ _ _ _ _
5. _ _ _ _ _ _ _ _ _ _ _ _ _

WHAT DO THESE THINGS HAVE IN COMMON?

What are your gifts?

1. _ _ _ _ _ _ _ _ _ _ _ _ _
2. _ _ _ _ _ _ _ _ _ _ _ _ _
3. _ _ _ _ _ _ _ _ _ _ _ _ _
4. _ _ _ _ _ _ _ _ _ _ _ _ _
5. _ _ _ _ _ _ _ _ _ _ _ _ _

What are favourite colours? Favourite art materials?

1. _ _ _ _ _ _ _ _ _ _ _ _ _
2. _ _ _ _ _ _ _ _ _ _ _ _ _
3. _ _ _ _ _ _ _ _ _ _ _ _ _
4. _ _ _ _ _ _ _ _ _ _ _ _ _
5. _ _ _ _ _ _ _ _ _ _ _ _ _

What writers really matter?

1. _ _ _ _ _ _ _ _ _ _ _ _ _
2. _ _ _ _ _ _ _ _ _ _ _ _ _
3. _ _ _ _ _ _ _ _ _ _ _ _ _
4. _ _ _ _ _ _ _ _ _ _ _ _ _
5. _ _ _ _ _ _ _ _ _ _ _ _ _

I cut up my sheet of things I was in love with and rearranged the pieces. There's room for you to try this at the back of the book.

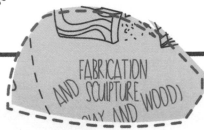

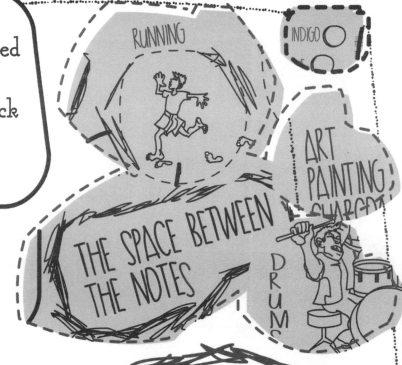

WHAT WAS IT I REALLY WANTED? AND WHY?

BY PUTTING DATES ON THNGS, I STARTED TO NOTICE PATTERNS. EVERYTHING THAT I HAPPENED TO LOVE WAS ANCIENT.

RUNNING, WRESTLING THE OLDEST SPORTS. WE'VE BEEN DRAWING AND PAINTING SINCE BEFORE THE ICE AGE. EVEN MY FAVOURITE PIGMENTS, AND TOOLS, AND MEDIUMS WERE ANCIENT.

I AM A CAVEMAN.
THIS WAS MY START.

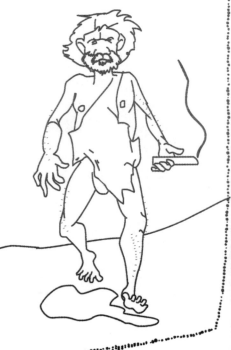

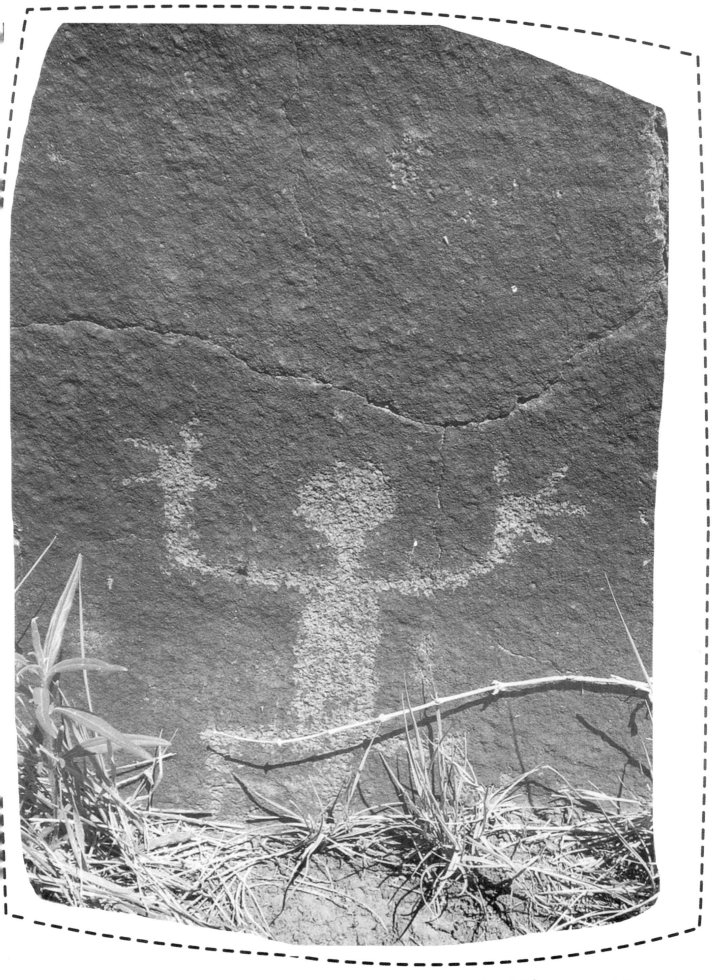

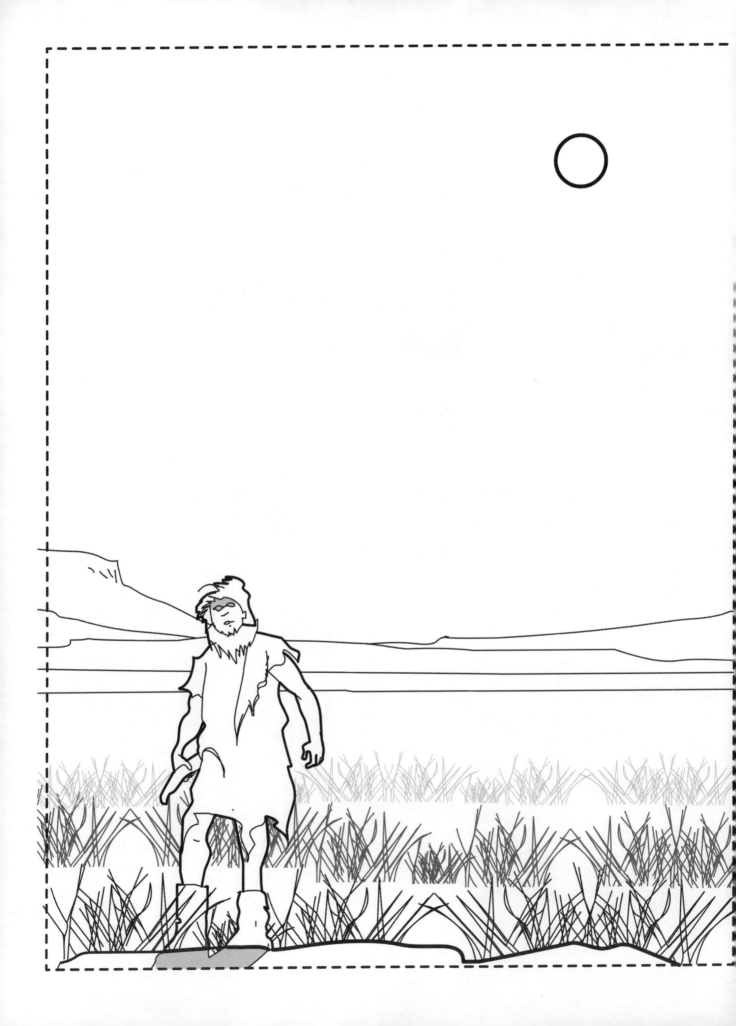

SURVIVAL ACTIVITY III

Finding your
tribe

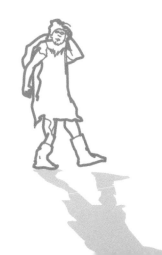

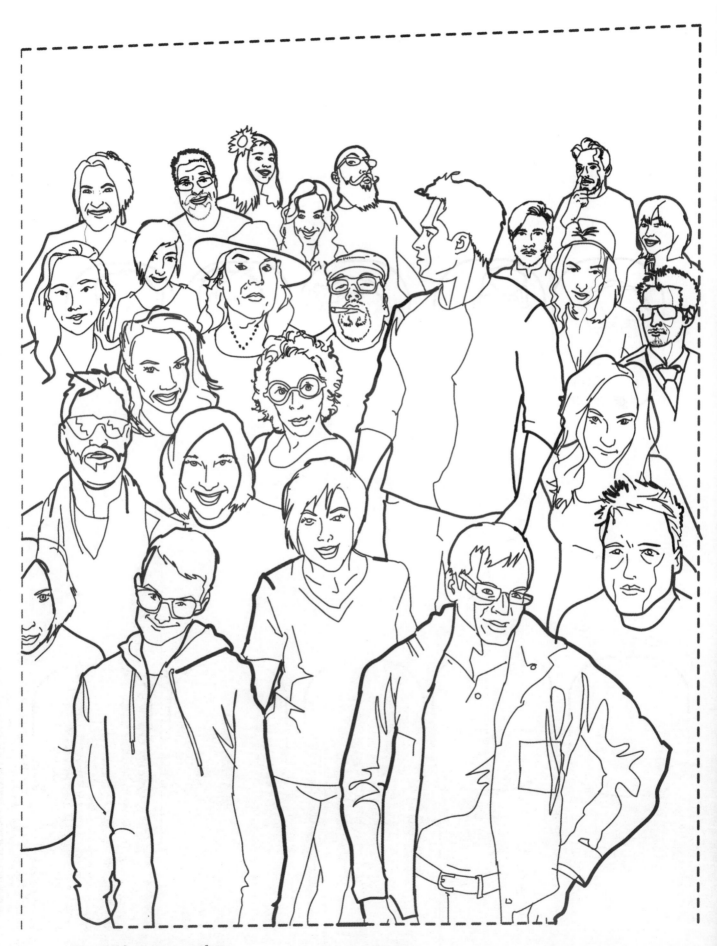

Once I knew I was a caveman, once I had a direction, I realized I was going to need to find my **family/gang** and a **tribe.**

This wasn't a question about who was my pal, but who were my crew?
I decided to try and fill my crew with **BOY BAND** archetypes, or rather something you'd see from a heist movie.

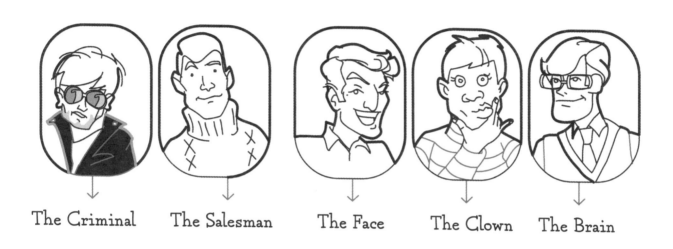

The Criminal   The Salesman   The Face   The Clown   The Brain

Who is in YOUR crew? And what do they do?

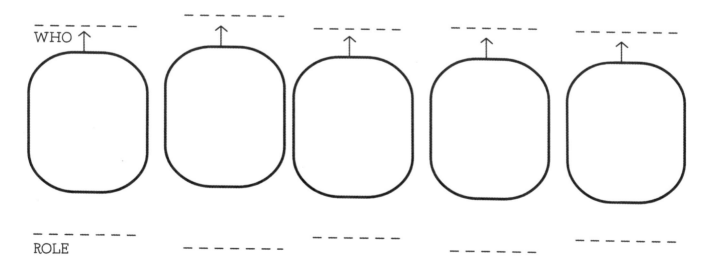

WHO

ROLE

It always blew my mind that F. Scott Fitzgerald and Ernest Hemingway and Ford Madox Ford and Gertrude Stein were friends; or how the five Dog Town kids turned out to be the best skateboarders in the world. How Truman Capote and Harper Lee were childhood friends, or how the Rat Packers evolved with Humphrey Bogart.

How did all these amazing world shakers grow up with best friends that turned out to be laterally predestined, equally implausible, world shakers...

These amazing pockets of possibility...

Finding your contemporaries

But they pushed each other.
They carved out that pocket.

They made a path and they all walked it together.
Like Mark Twain and his young friend, Helen Keller.

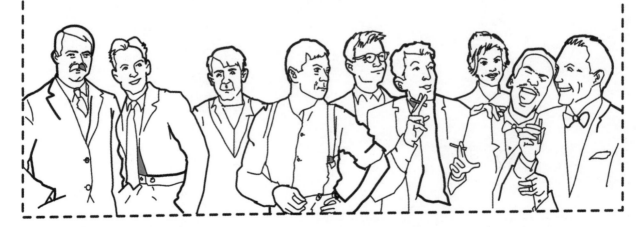

If you are going to embark on the hero's journey, there are eight Jungian archetypes to look for:

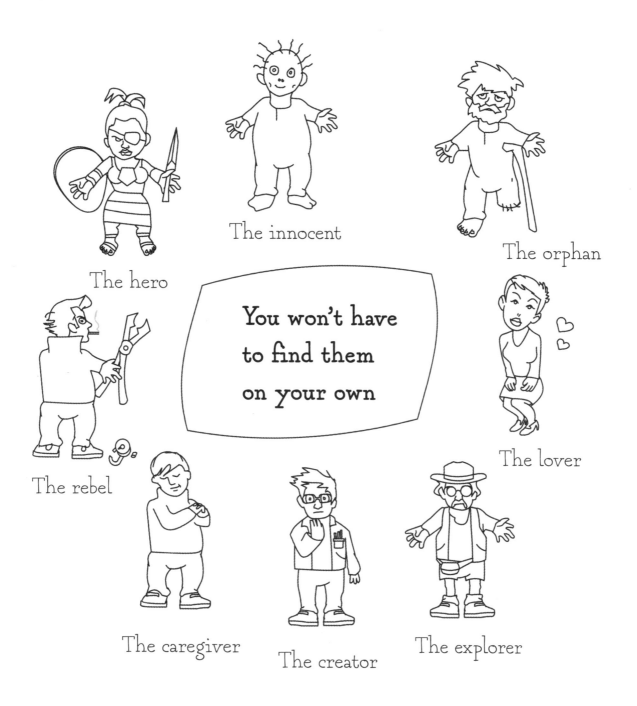

The innocent

The orphan

The hero

You won't have to find them on your own

The lover

The rebel

The caregiver

The creator

The explorer

Keep your eyes open. They will be looking for you.

Dad, is the world collapsing?

Yes, I guess it is.

How will painting
and making art help
in a zombie
apocalypse?

(Long Pause)

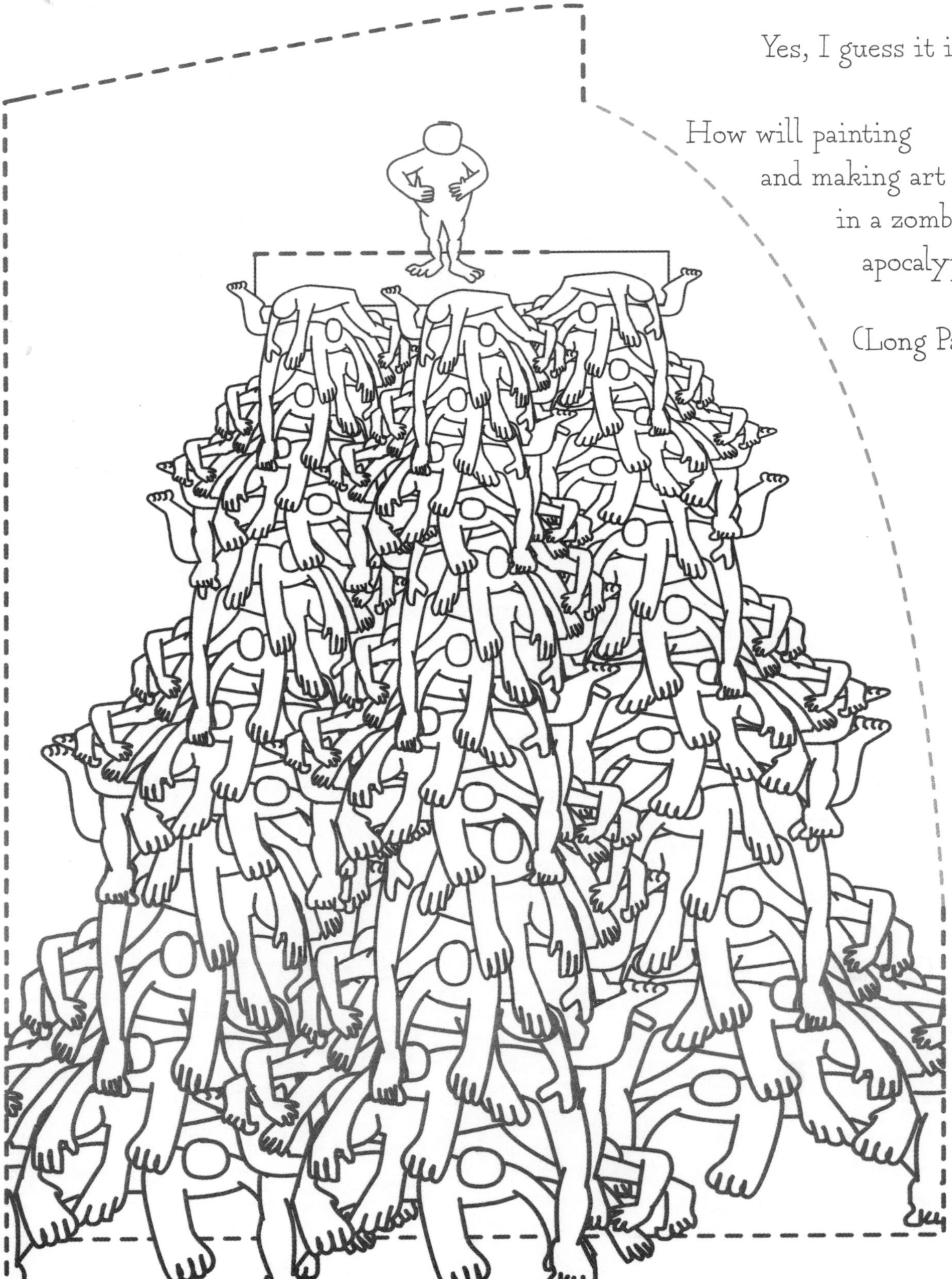

And even if I found my tribe
I needed a whole lot of
money.

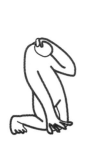 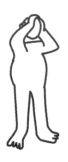 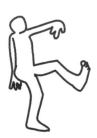

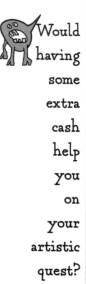

Would having some extra cash help you on your artistic quest?

You might not need a space but start thinking, if you had a space, where would it be?

Tower, boat, cube truck, tent, beach, the moon, downtown, shopping mall, church, school, old haunted house, warehouse, house, garage, friend's house, parent's house, travelling cart, bicycle cart, pub, bar, coffee shop, laundromat, tanning salon, library, university, TEDx, train station, bus station, bathrooms, in an old fashioned phone booth, in a shed, in an alley, in the space between two old buildings, vestibules, lobbies, hotels, office building, government building, shanty town, the country, the park, on an airplane, cruise ship, outside the grocery store, parking lots, in a castle, under a bridge, at your grandma's cottage, **in a rocket?**... I could go on. Or maybe you should go on:

_____

_____

_____

_____

_____

_____

_____

_____

_____

See it, smell it, draw it, just start carving out an image of the space you want to be in. Forget about money and just picture the kind of lighting you want. What city is it in? What are the doors and windows like? Cut up pictures or draw it, but you have to find a way to see the space you need to be in.

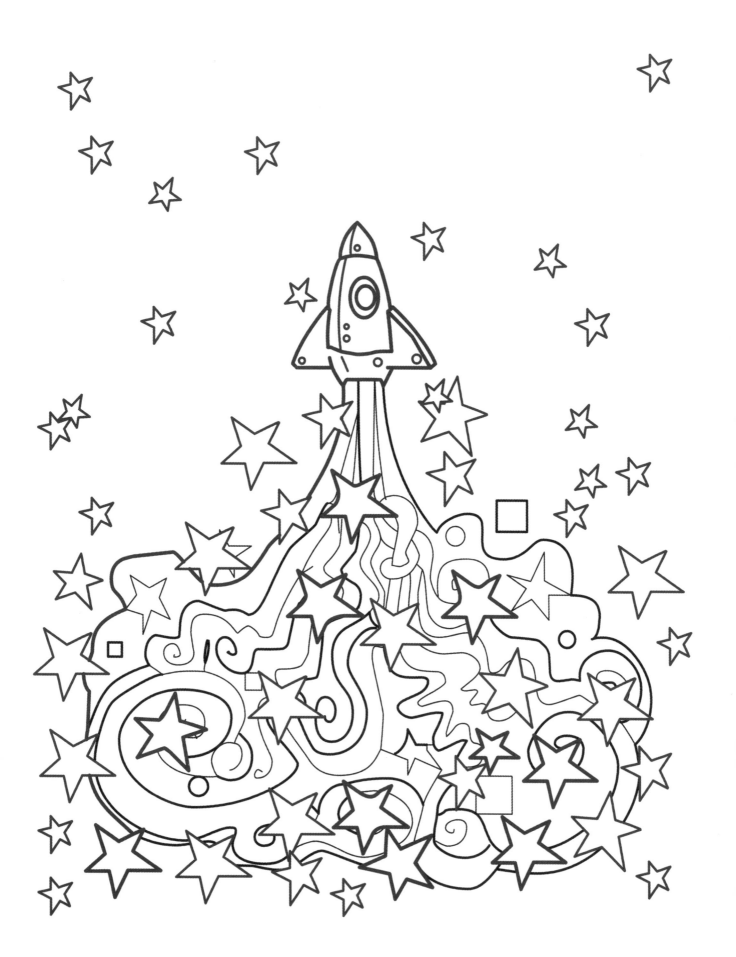

Try and draw your space into these boxes, the working lines should help you with the perspective. Top view is cool too, if you don't like perspective drawings.

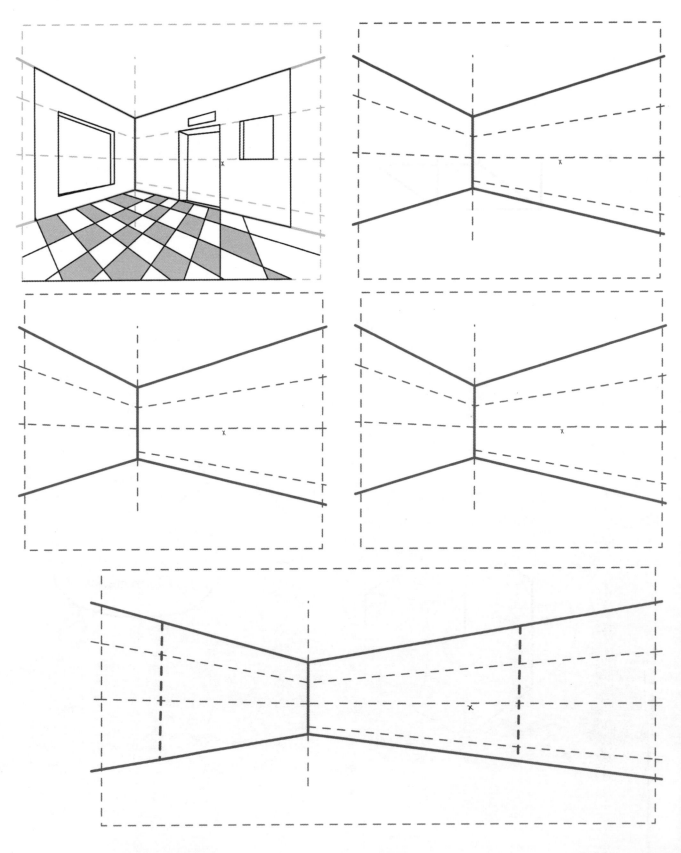

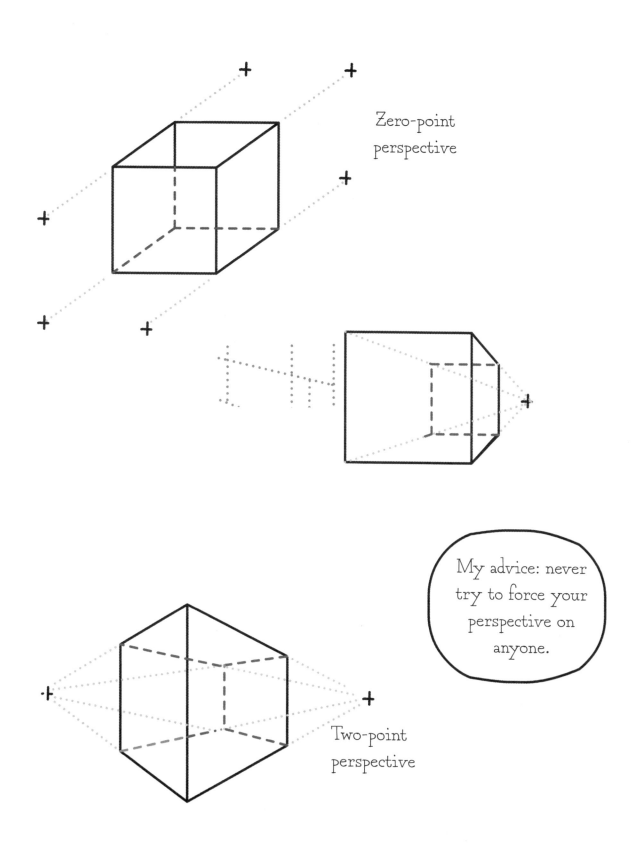

Zero-point
perspective

My advice: never
try to force your
perspective on
anyone.

Two-point
perspective

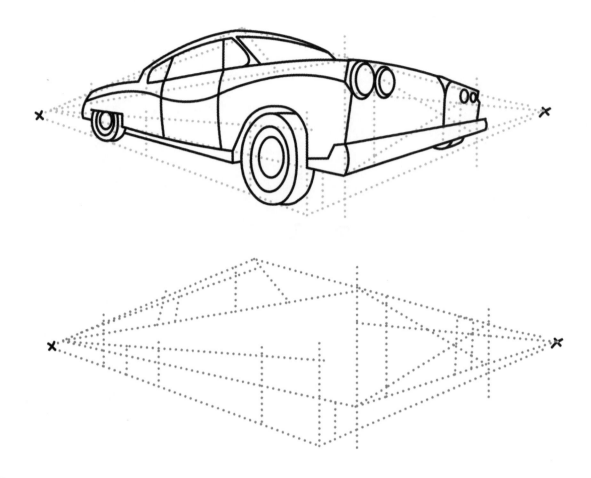

Try
to
draw
Rich's
kind of
car here
or any
kind of
car you
want.

SURVIVAL ACTIVITY IV

Establish

permanence

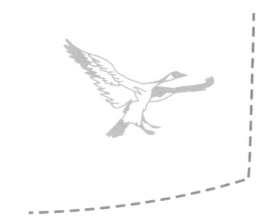

I found a building. It was $3,000 a month. I wanted a three-month lease and I knew it was possible because it had been a campaign office on a three-month lease.

(If you are looking for a pop up, keep an eye out for a political campaign office. Somehow politicians seem to get three-month campaign headquarters every election.)

The landlord didn't care what we did to the building because they expected to demolish it. Otherwise (for the area), it would have been $10,000 a month. I wanted three months. The landlord wanted three years. Three years would have been a $100,000 contract. I had $4,000 and hoped to earn at least $5,000 over the summer.

None of this seemed to matter because the landlord thought I was a nut and he had no intention of renting to me anyway. We met and I asked for a three-month lease, and he said that was impossible (which I knew was a lie). So at first he said, "NO." But then he said, "NO WAY!"

Each time we met he was more emphatic but I kept buying him coffee and he kept meeting me for coffee. We met a few times and he said, "NO, NO, NO!"

This was all fine because I didn't have the money anyway.

Finally, and I was sure this was going to be the last time I met with him, I ran into a lady I just happened to recognize from the campaign office.

She was on her way to drop off the keys to the landlord, which is probably why he agreed to meet me for coffee.

I asked the lady for a favour and said, "Would you say to the landlord, IS IT TRUE RICH THEROUX MIGHT BE TAKING OVER THIS SPACE?!"

An hour later I sign a three-month lease.

Now all I need is $9,000.

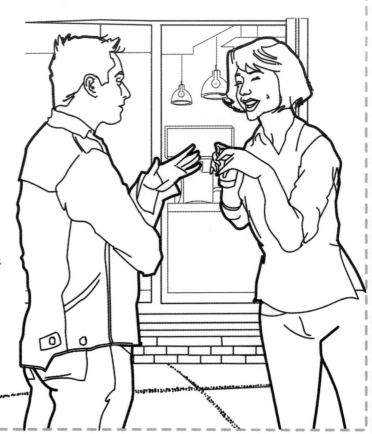

Sometimes things just work out.

There isn't much surplus from my teaching salary and I don't have any savings, but I've been kicking around this seed of an idea for almost 20 years. If I can find $5,000 in the space by the end of the summer, I'll be okay. But I need almost half of that still for the deposit.

I need a few grand. I need it with all my heart.

I need, need, need it.

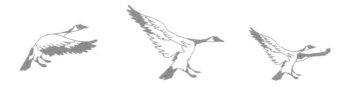

And just like that, I get a call to do some emergency illustrations for a book.

I don't sleep for two weeks, but then I get a cheque.

And keys to my building on the first day of summer.

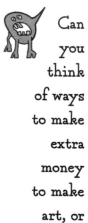 Can you think of ways to make extra money to make art, or die?

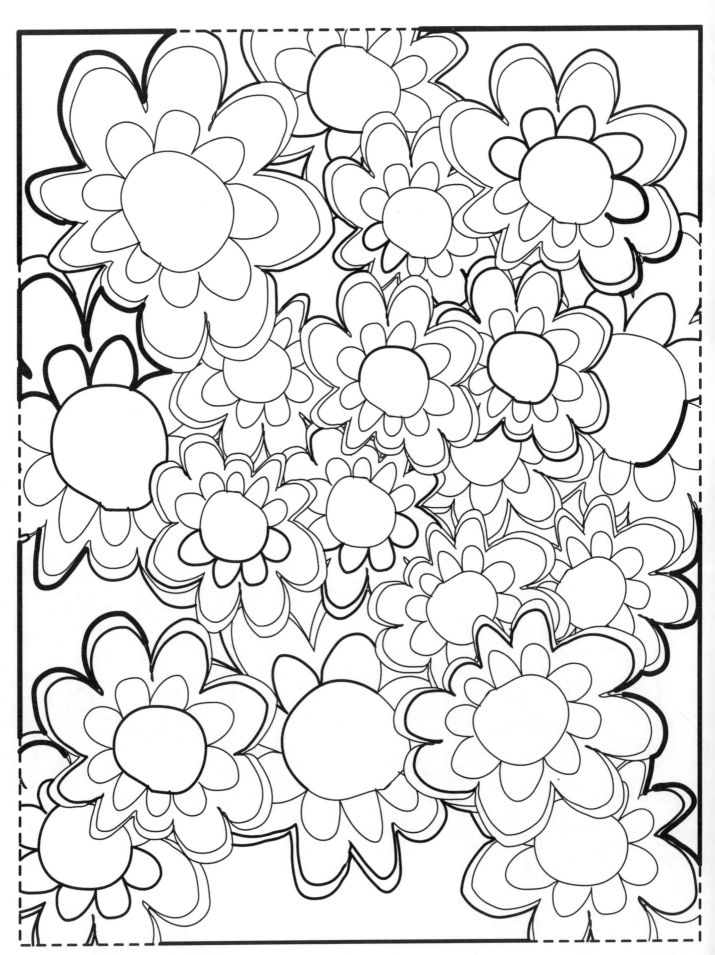

To find low rent, it's not uncommon for artists to have to take over spaces that no one in their right mind wants. You don't have to live like this, but you do have to become super handy, really fast.

We work 11 days straight to get the place cleaned up, with virtually no rest.

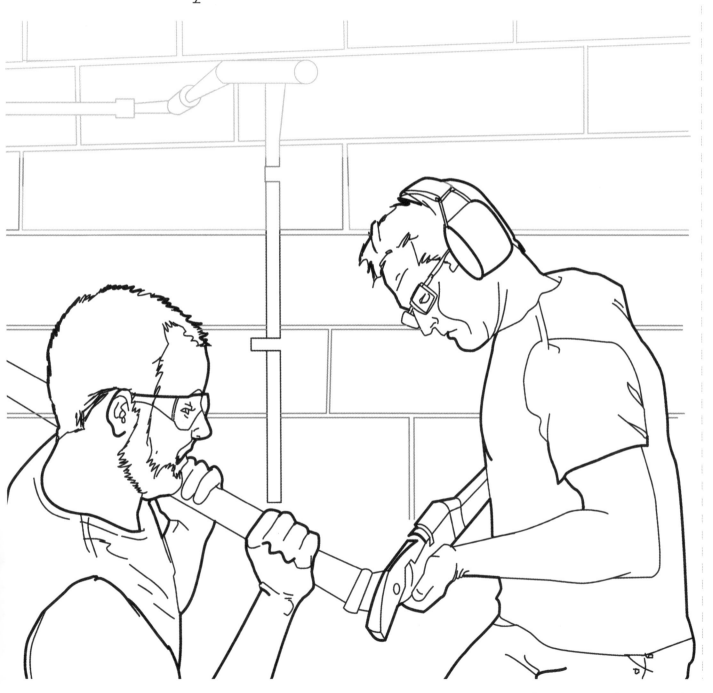

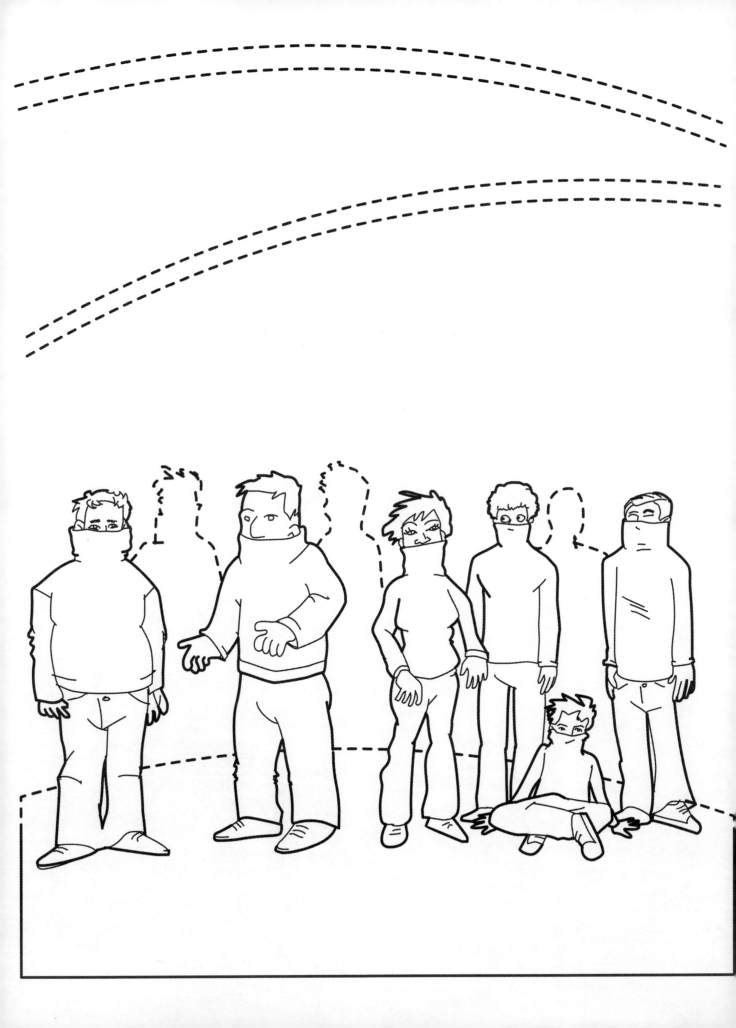

SURVIVAL ACTIVITY V

The urge to

communicate

The chance of being born

was astronomical

astronomical

and born here

with talent

and some food

and by HERE I mean

just far enough from the sun

that all the water didn't

boil off the earth

astronomical

the chance at

this life

every painful moment

not to be taken lightly

life isn't fair

your advantage

was absolute

please eat

this day

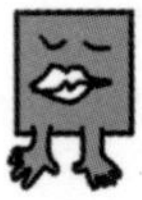

Can you try writing your own poem about eating up a day?

One of our first artists to hang her art drops off her work and attached is a copy of her artist statement. I have to admit, it is a shock. We opened our own space so we wouldn't have to do things like write artist statements.

"Do we need artist statements?" Elijah asks.

"I don't have one, do you?"

We rush to our studios and have the

WORLD'S GREATEST
ARTIST
STATEMENT
contest.

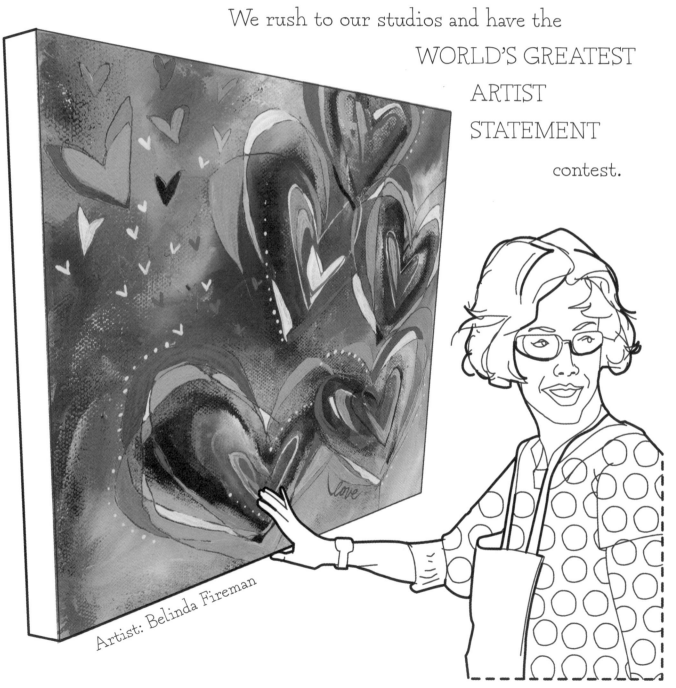

Artist: Belinda Fireman

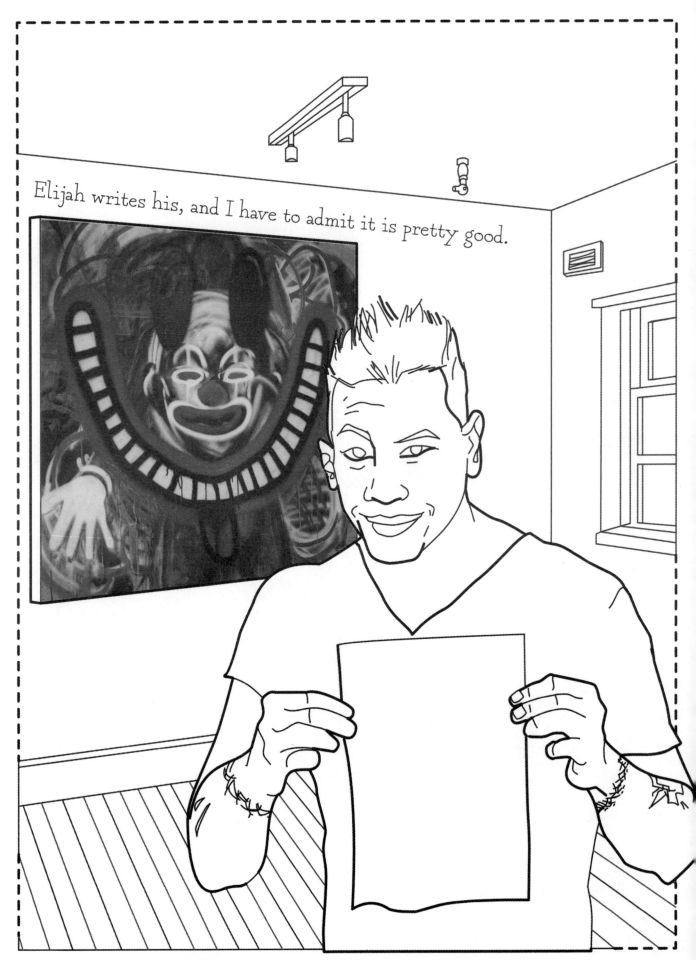

Elijah writes his, and I have to admit it is pretty good.

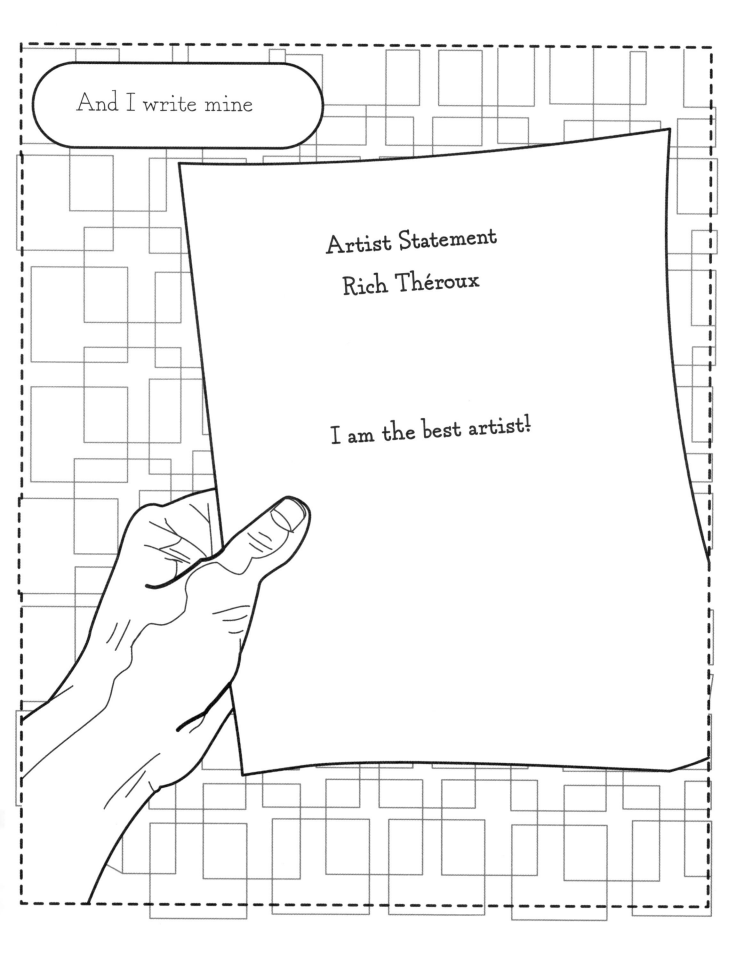

And I write mine

Artist Statement

Rich Théroux

I am the best artist!

Why do we need an Artist Statement?

It's the document we use to tell people about our art. It's the document that explains what our show is about. It's the reason why we should have a show. It's why the government should give us a grant. It is what we want people to understand about our work.

My art is the best art.

My show is about the best artist.

I should have a show because I'm the best artist.

The government should give me a grant because I am the best artist. Please understand I'm the best artist.

I should say I am being funny. It's a lot funnier when you're on the losing end of things. I'm not the best artist. I'm actually kind of an tomato can. That could just as easily be my artist statement.

I sit down with Bruce Watson who teaches a course on how to write an artist statement at the local polytechnic.

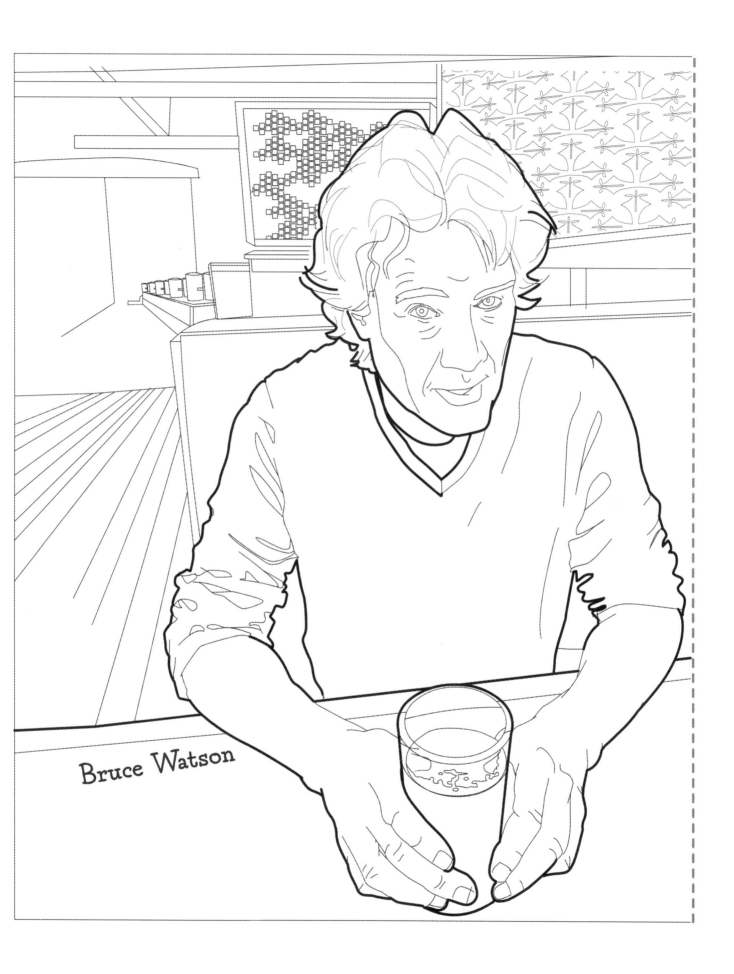

Bruce Watson

BRUCE SAYS: If you give artists a piece of paper, they'll draw on it. If you ask them to write, they'll get angry. Artists tend not to be writers, so one thing I tell people about writing an artist statement is to speak it out naturally instead of writing it first.

One of the problems is that too many artists start writing artist statements too soon: you need a whole bunch of art before you can write a good artist statement, otherwise you're just making stuff up. There is also this (grimace) antagonistic relationship between people writing artist statements and the people they are writing them to, like it's some kind of con job. We all have to try and get over that.

An artist statement has got to be honest. When I'm teaching, the first thing I do is ask people to ground themselves in the materials. That's the part we really love, that's where the honesty comes from. Once you have that down, you can start asking, WHY? We like how it smells; we like how it feels; so ground the language in that first.

Another thing is to talk the artist statement out with your mom.

Tell your mom why she should like your paintings. Tell her what you want her to notice about your work. If you can say, "Look mom, look what I did with that paint stroke," and then tell her why you love that paint stroke, then you can really start to understand something about your own work.

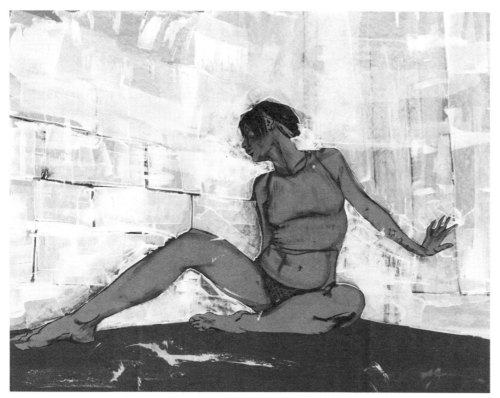

What I love most about charcoal is the pitch of it. I love the way the black sucks the light. I also love to sketch on wood. I use the grain as something to push against.

What are the materials, the smells, the tools that you love?

My go-to materials are: on/using:

1. _____
2. _____
3. _____
4. _____
5. _____
6. _____
7. _____
8. _____
9. _____
10.

My Artist Statement

Boy, have an idea
It's free, let's go.
Don't sit, it will seep out
and impregnate someone else.

Draw. Write. Shape. Sculpt.

Shove or let go? Shove!
Find a space
Big, bright, and dirty.
If no one would set foot inside it's for you.

Pull down walls
(the ragged ones in the basement).
Pull down fences and make the whole thing free.

Clean. Scrub. Paint.

There's 13 drug needles in the parking lot.
Those are your security deposit.
Dumpster after dumpster.
Hug. Kiss. Whisper.

It's yours as long as you can pinch a fist.
Fight. Boy you'll paint with one hand
and ball the other.

Crazy people need love too
and they get rough.
Be rough boy,
be rough and gentle,
and don't get hurt.

Keep the little ones safe, pretty girls and rich people and that
guy with no pants, and the gaping crowd, it's scary
throwing out those needles.
Be scary boy. This old building is coming down so you can rent it.
Keep it clean. Not too clean mind you.
Keep it safe. Keep it beautiful. Take a risk boy.
Have me. I'm yours.

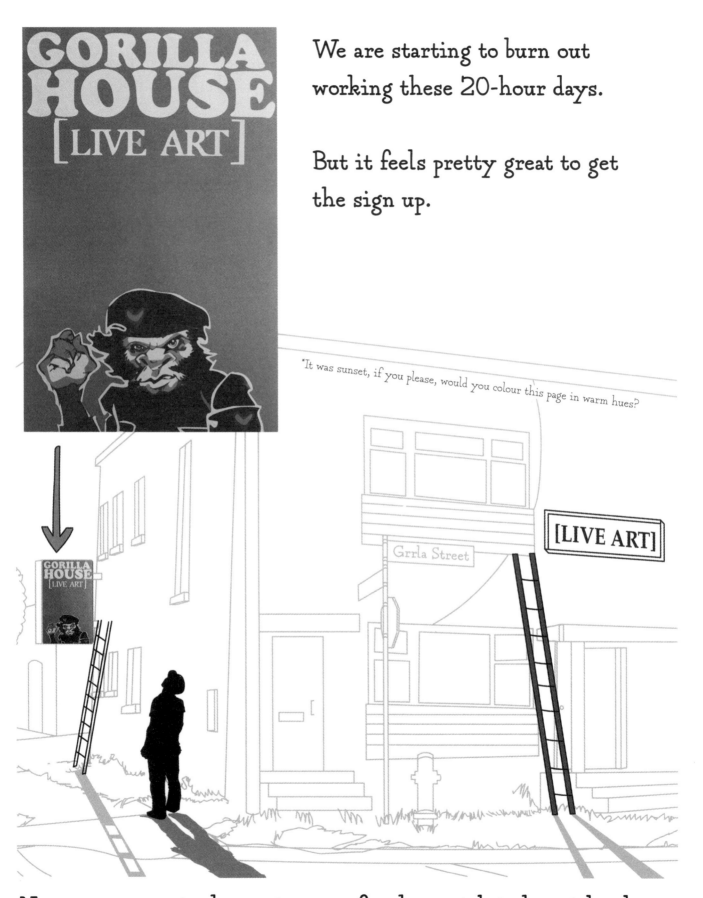

GORILLA HOUSE [LIVE ART]

We are starting to burn out working these 20-hour days.

But it feels pretty great to get the sign up.

*It was sunset, if you please, would you colour this page in warm hues?

Grrla Street

[LIVE ART]

No one ever noticed my sign was fixed on with industrial velcro.

I was going to call the place "Battles Cafe." My plan was to sell coffee and scones to moms during afternoon art lessons.

However, the building we find is unfit for serving food. Earlier that year I bought my son and me matching father and son gorilla suits (which may have eventually lead to my divorce) but I reckon I can use the studio as an excuse to write off the gorilla suits. And so I name it

GORILLA HOUSE.

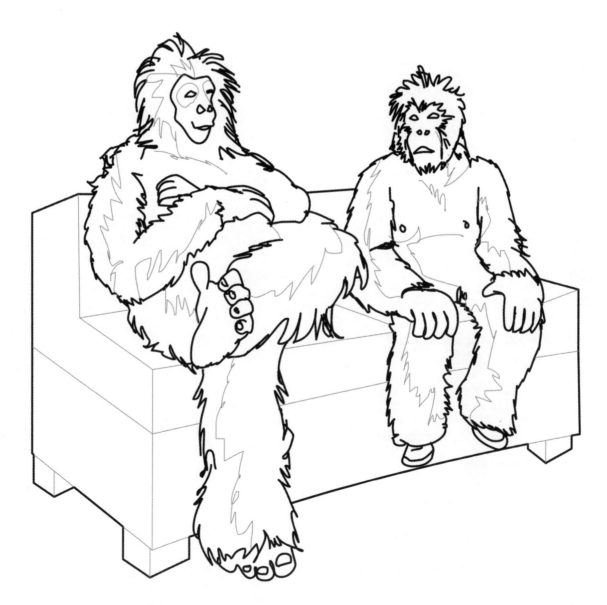

I'm lucky.

I'd worked as a media and graphic designer, so I could put together a lot of the business stuff on my own. Here are a couple of things that work out in my favour:

I'm intentionally vague. It works because we have limited space.

I need a steady stream of wild people wandering in but never too many at once. Radio ads are out of the question but a big purple gorilla on the side of the building brings in the curious and imaginative people.

Our branding is a Rebel Gorilla but our logo is this funny little heart.

The heart is easy to reproduce and is instantly recognizable.

The sum of this is a purple gorilla with a wild heart insignia.

A killer logo is probably one of the few things you might consider hiring someone to do for you.

Avoid being too timely or too clever because clever jokes run thin really quickly.

Your branding needs to live on your skin and in your ear and on everything you touch.

It's going to be your new everywhere.

We make stickers out of the hearts and people stick them everywhere.

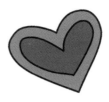

These's room right here to try out some logos that might become your own brand.

Once you have designed a logo that you can live with for a long time, make sure it starts out in the computer as a vector.

[Please don't be insulted if I explain vectors, I want you to know how I made this book as well as logos.]

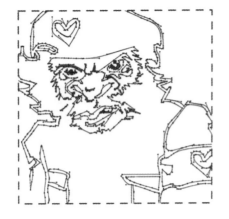

Vector graphics are made out of shapes. The computer knows there are nodes or points and the computer knows the shape of the arc between the nodes and that's what makes the shapes into an image.

Because of this, vector graphics use very little memory and disk space and they are simple enough for a computer to cut out with a blade on a plotter.

Also, you can print the images any size and they'll stay sharp. You can do whatever you want to your base logo with filters and computer programs but make your base art work vector.

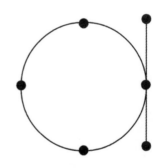

This circle only needs a few bits of information, there are four points, and the arcs are even and that makes a circle. There are only a few points in this circle.

*Vector images are a little bit like layers of cut paper.

Bit map images are the images you usually see on the computer. If you look really closely, they are made out of tiny little blocks and each block has one more bit of information. They are limited to the resolution they are made in, they get chunky as you blow them up.

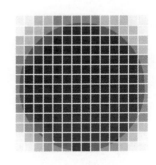

*Bit map images are almost more like embroidery.

The secret meanings of lines and shapes

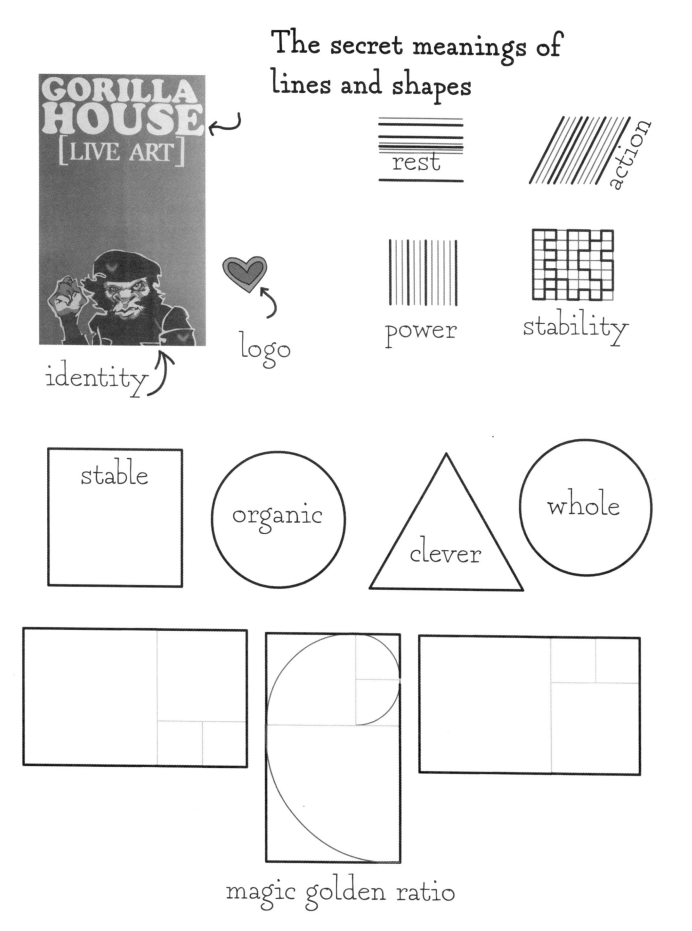

GORILLA HOUSE [LIVE ART]

identity

logo

rest

action

power

stability

stable

organic

clever

whole

magic golden ratio

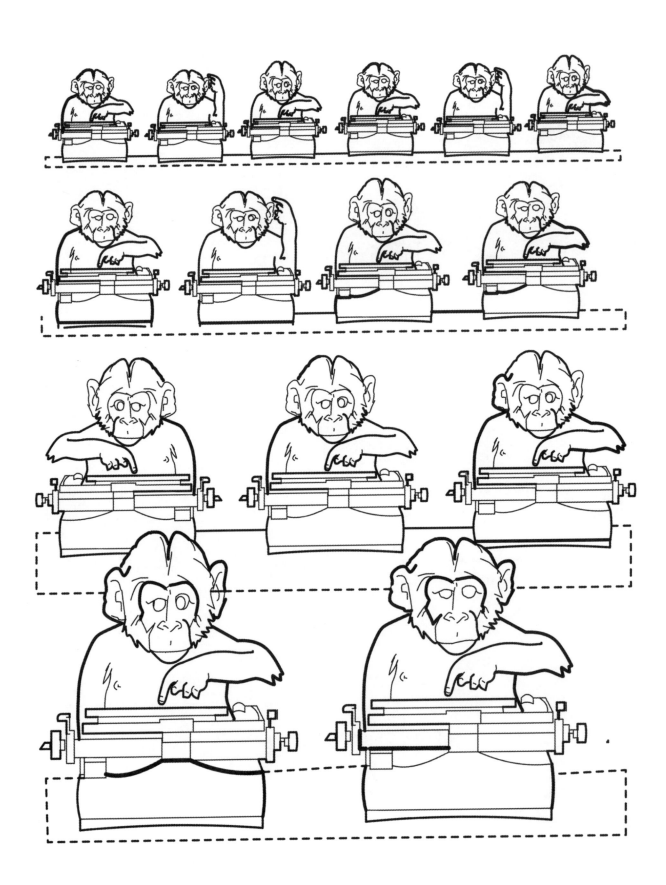

SURVIVAL ACTIVITIES VI

Losing control

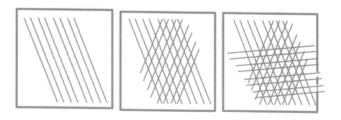

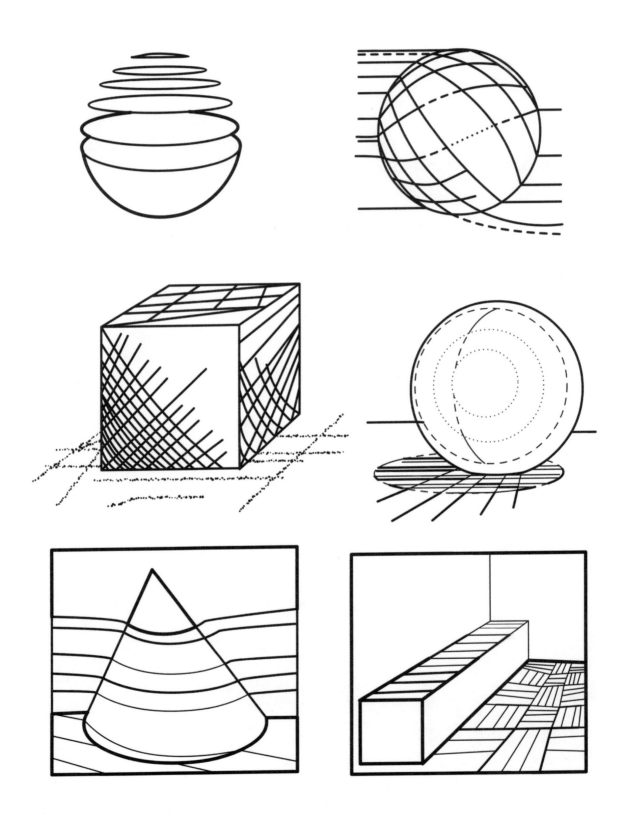

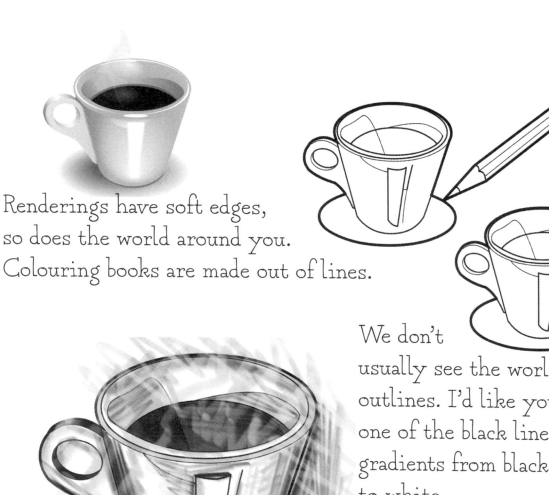

Renderings have soft edges,
so does the world around you.
Colouring books are made out of lines.

We don't
usually see the world as
outlines. I'd like you to take
one of the black lines and shade
gradients from black to grey
to white.

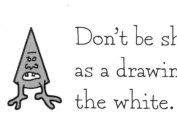

Don't be shy to use your eraser
as a drawing tool, to draw back
the white.

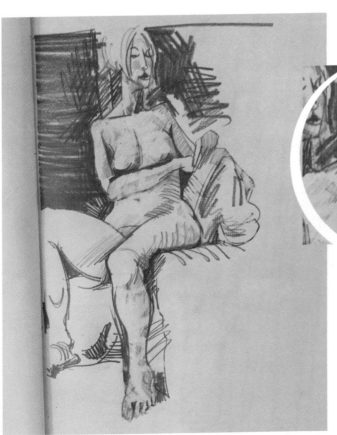

Quality of Line is a pain to describe with words but it's pretty easy to understand visually.

It's the sense that the line has variety and a level of intention, looseness and control. If you rotate your pencil in your hand, just a half turn every few strokes, you will keep the tip sharp.

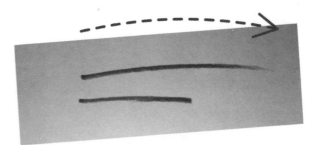

Sometimes your stroke goes off into space and fades away.

 Try fading it away here.

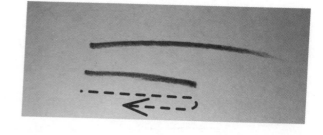

Sometimes you might shoot it backwards to hide your tracks,

 Try shooting your stoke backwards.

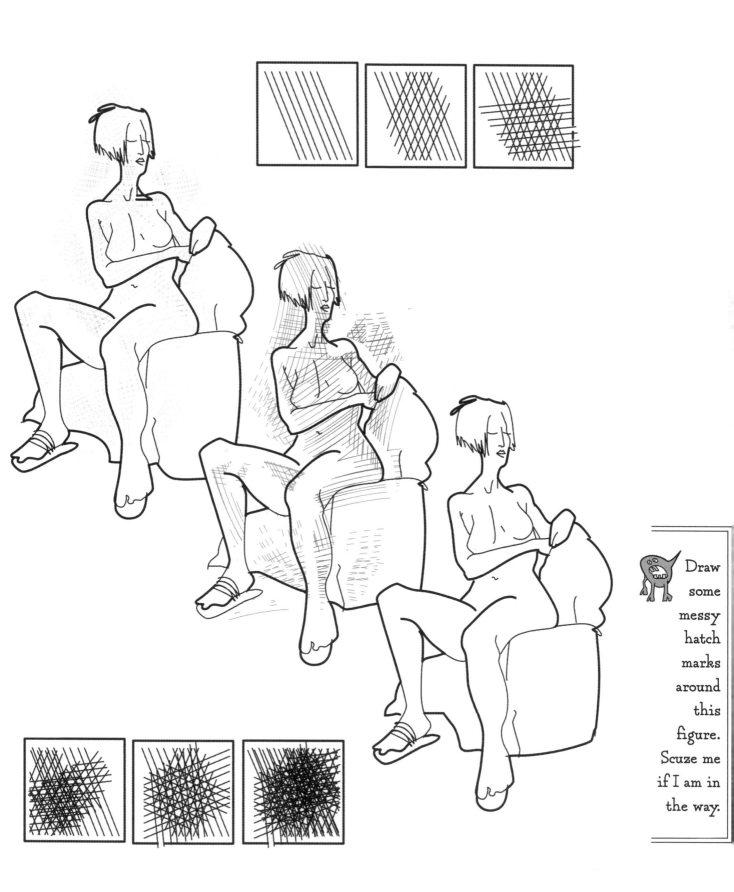

Draw some messy hatch marks around this figure. Scuze me if I am in the way.

*9	*9	*9	*9	*9	*9	*9	*9	*9	*9
*9	*5	*5	*5	*5	*5	*5	*5	*5	*9
*9	*5	*4	*4	*4	*4	*4	*4	*5	*9
*9	*5	*4	*3	*3	*3	*3	*4	*5	*9
*9	*5	*4	*3	*2	*2	*3	*4	*5	*9
*9	*5	*4	*3	*2	*2	*3	*4	*5	*9
*9	*5	*4	*3	*3	*3	*3	*4	*5	*9
*9	*5	*4	*4	*4	*4	*4	*4	*5	*9
*9	*5	*5	*5	*5	*5	*5	*5	*5	*9
*9	*9	*9	*9	*9	*9	*9	*9	*9	*9

*2	*2	*2	*2	*2	*2	*2	*2	*2	*2
*2	*3	*3	*3	*3	*3	*3	*3	*3	*2
*2	*3	*4	*4	*4	*4	*4	*4	*3	*2
*2	*3	*4	*5	*5	*5	*5	*4	*3	*2
*2	*3	*4	*5	*9	*9	*5	*4	*3	*2
*2	*3	*4	*5	*9	*9	*5	*4	*3	*2
*2	*3	*4	*5	*5	*5	*5	*4	*3	*2
*2	*3	*4	*4	*4	*4	*4	*4	*3	*2
*2	*3	*3	*3	*3	*3	*3	*3	*3	*2
*2	*2	*2	*2	*2	*2	*2	*2	*2	*2

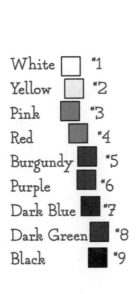

White ☐ *1
Yellow ☐ *2
Pink ◼ *3
Red ◼ *4
Burgundy ◼ *5
Purple ◼ *6
Dark Blue ◼ *7
Dark Green ◼ *8
Black ◼ *9

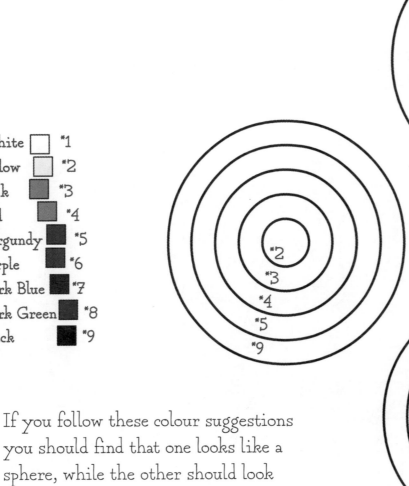

*2
*3
*4
*5
*9

*9
*5
*4
*3
*2

If you follow these colour suggestions you should find that one looks like a sphere, while the other should look like a bowl.

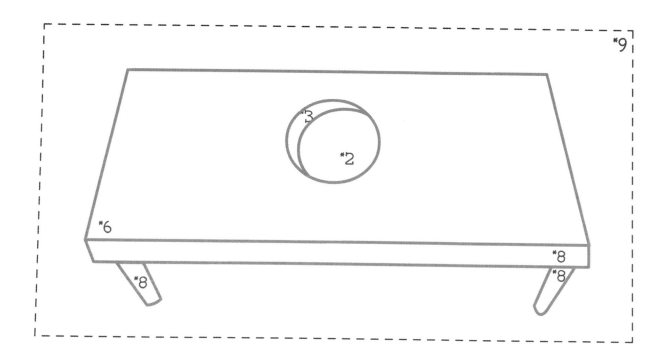

Depending on how you colour these two tables, one will look like a hole in the table and the other will look like a ball.

[feel free to prove me wrong]

White ☐ *1
Yellow ☐ *2
Pink ☐ *3
Red ☐ *4
Burgundy ■ *5
Purple ■ *6
Dark Blue ■ *7
Dark Green ■ *8
Black ■ *9

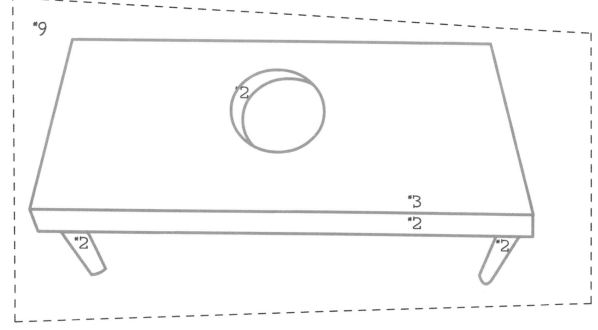

When you are looking at something under a warm light, try using cool colours in the shadows.

However, when you are showing a cool light, try using warmer hues in the shadow areas.

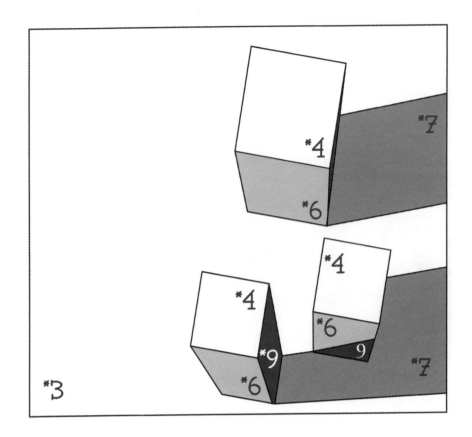

White   *1
Yellow   *2
Pink   *3
Red   *4
Burgundy   *5
Purple   *6
Dark Blue   *7
Dark Green   *8
Black   *9

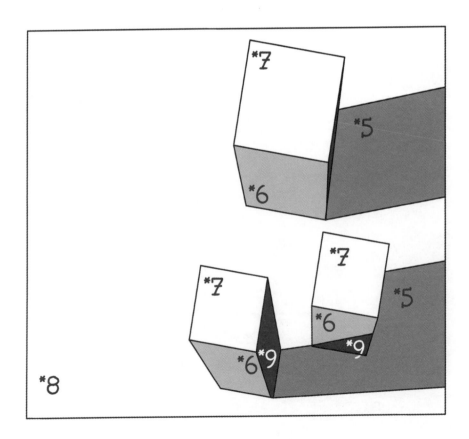

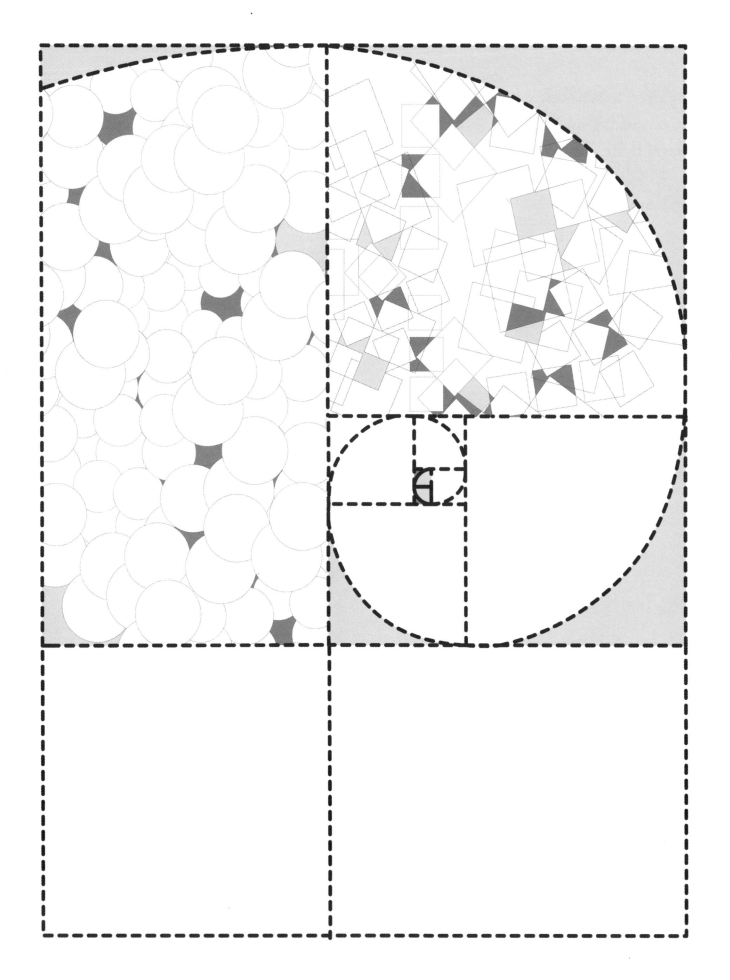

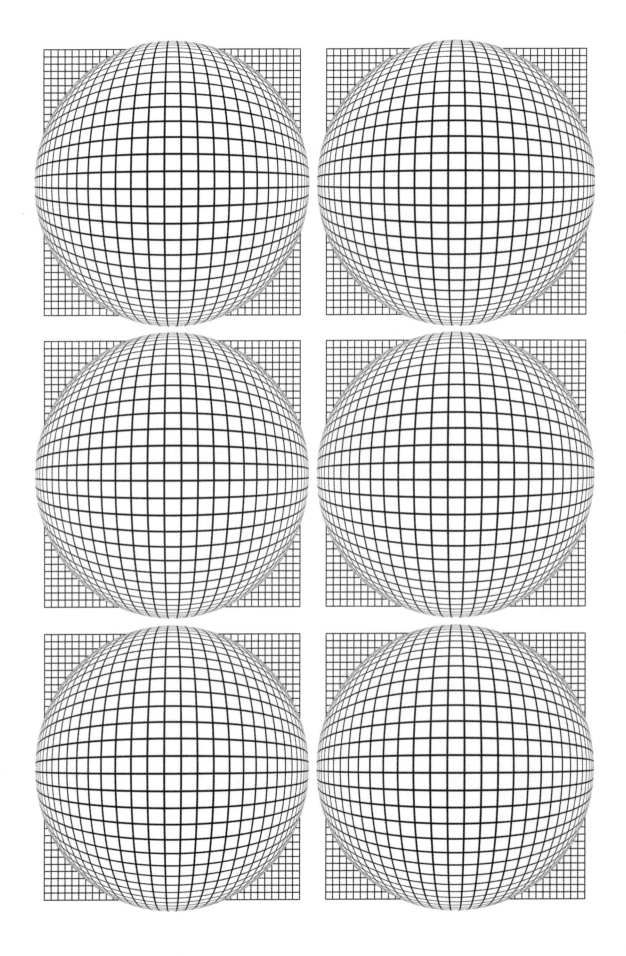

Search for
quality

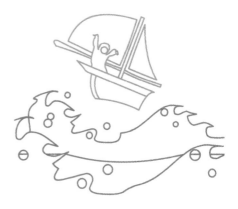

Don't talk to

the blank canvas

Don't plead don't

make threats

See it

Kill it

Re-animate

Kill it again

but don't talk to it

don't give it a name

don't give it

a chance

to breathe

Kill it

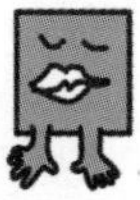

Can you write a poem where you totally kill it and then re-animate?

Damn, I wanted something so badly, it was just behind my eyelids. I knew I'd know it when I saw it.

I wanted a place where people could share art making with the public. I envisioned someone walking to work and seeing one of us stretching a canvas in the dark of morning; at noon walking by and seeing the canvas take shape and at the end of the day packing up to walk home and to see the work reveal itself under studio track lighting.

I wanted all the people who'd forgotten how to draw and paint to see the magic we do in the studio.

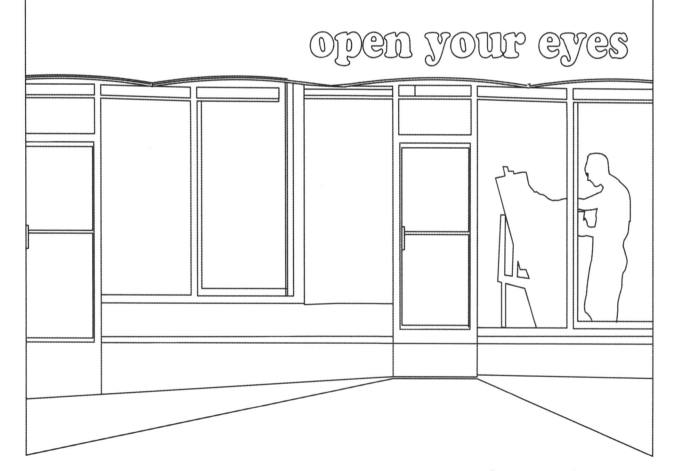

open your eyes

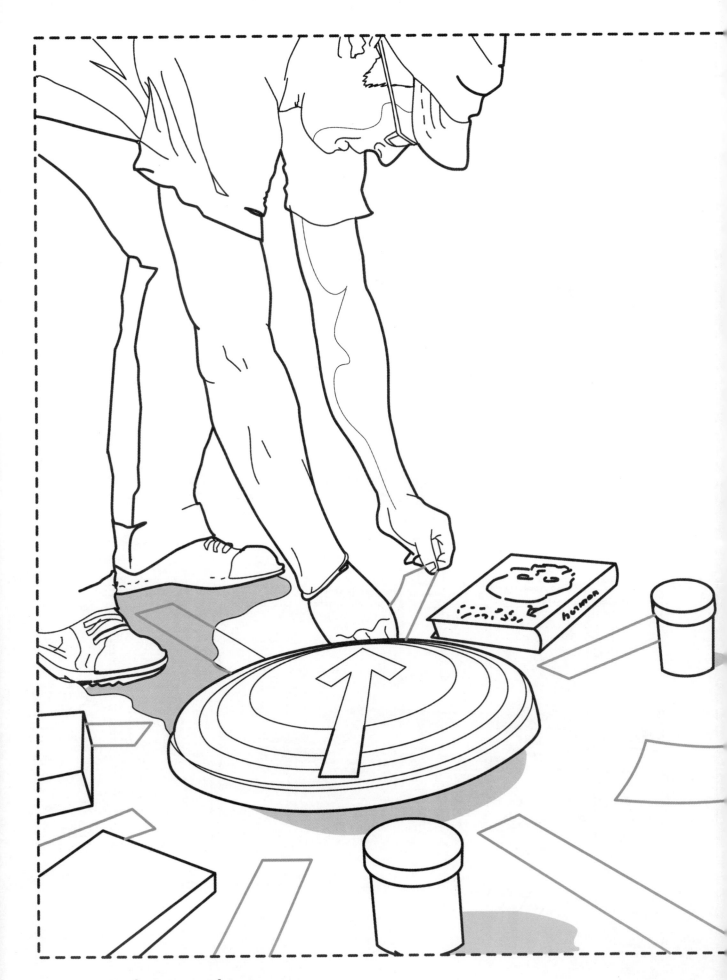

We are now ready to present the magic.

We have our soft opening on a Wednesday, two weeks into summer. Thursday night is normally art night — openings, happenings, events, but Wednesdays are dead to the world. We don't want to have art openings. We don't want rules, but we need to move bodies into the gallery.

The only thing I am sure of is that I want to put the art making into full view of the public.

GORILLA HOUSE LIVE ART.

Eight artists (THE PRIME EIGHT) walk in at seven o'clock, spin a wheel, pick three working art concepts, and paint for two hours.

We decide we will have an auction at nine.

No winners, no losers, no rules.

The wheel is an old Lazy Susan with special books and objects around it. We call it the wheel of doom.

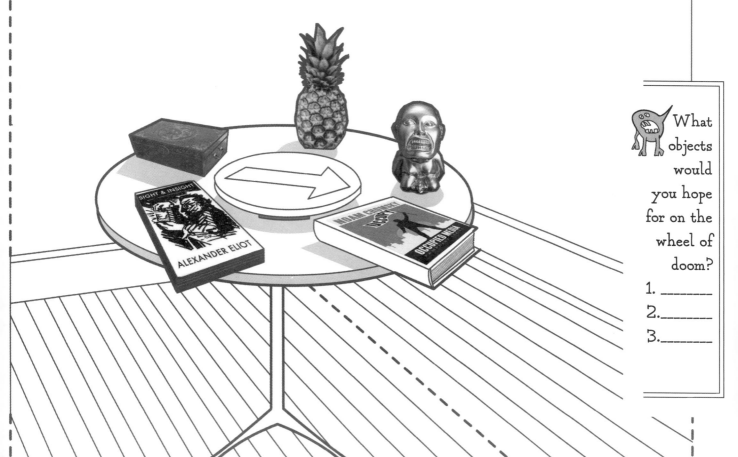

What objects would you hope for on the wheel of doom?

1. _____
2. _____
3. _____

We practice run the first event with just us. The eight prime artists, no audience, just us.

At nine o'clock we get to the part where we we'd planned to have an auction. What to do now? We have an auction. I start my first bid at 58 cents. The prime eight bid on the work and I sell my piece for $60. It was the most fun, most beautiful, most dear, thing I ever experienced.

I cried fat tears of joy.

We all did.

Forever was a long time to wait for this.

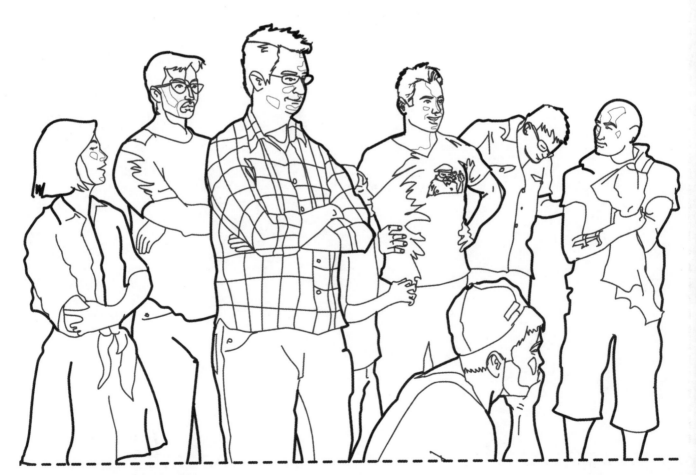

For the next week, we hustle the services of a host (I know he is a little loungy) but trust me, the host is essential. The host is your advocate. No matter what you say about yourself, people never listen.

What your host says about you will stick.
Treat your host well. The host is the BOSS.

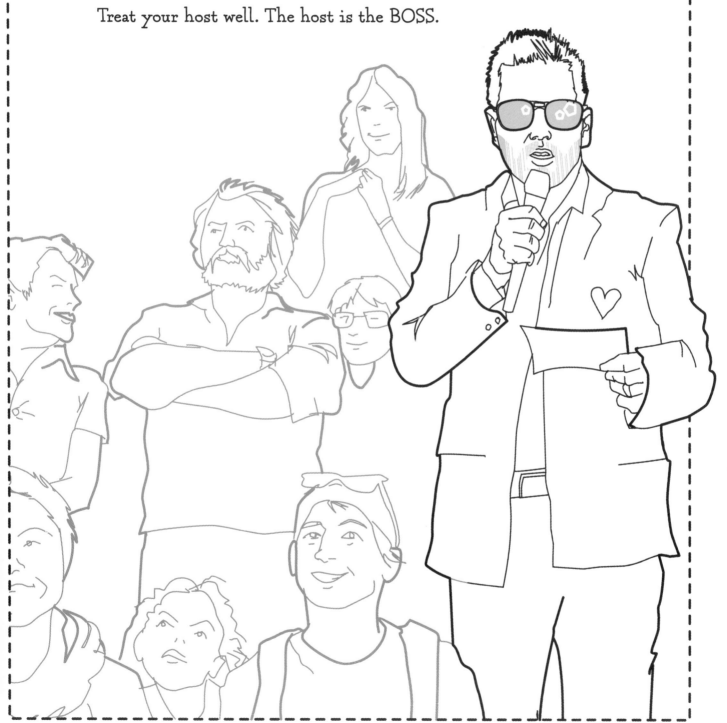

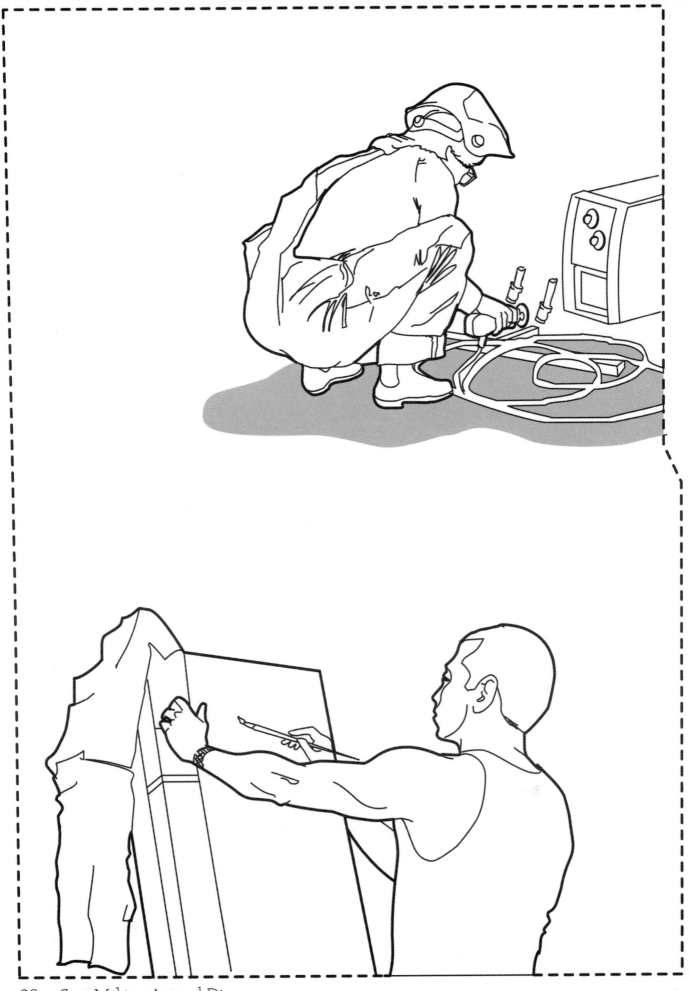

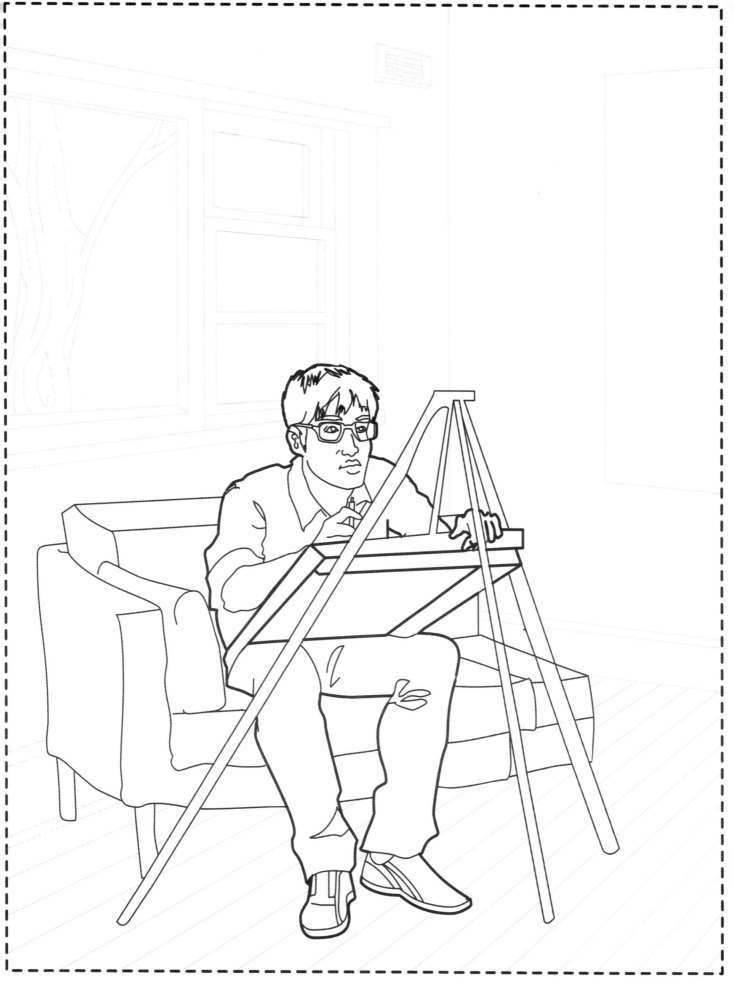

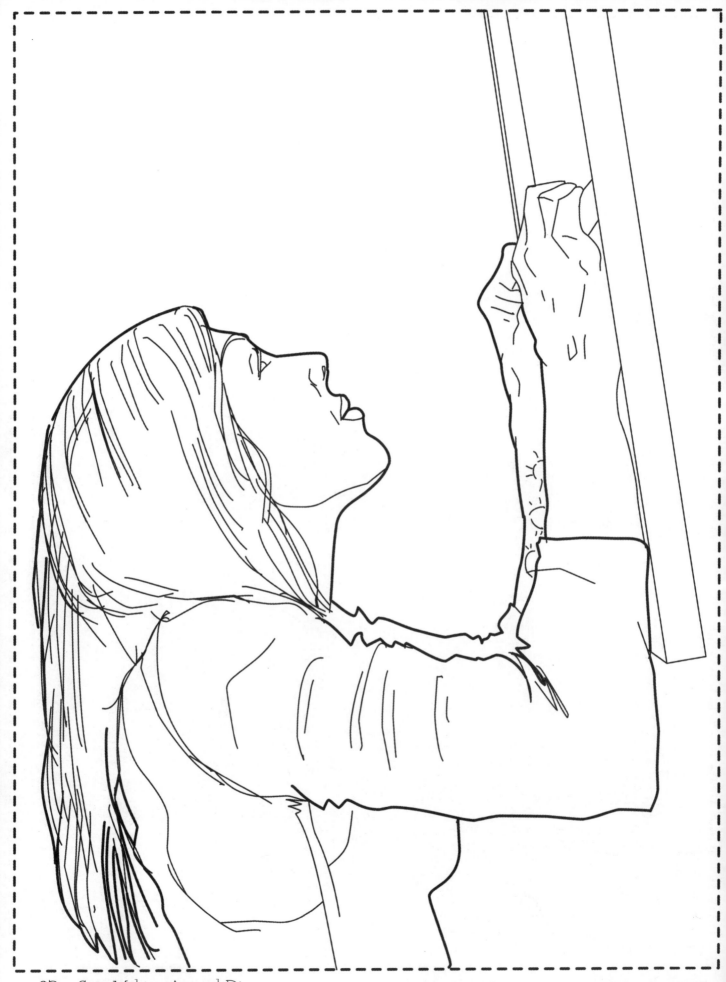

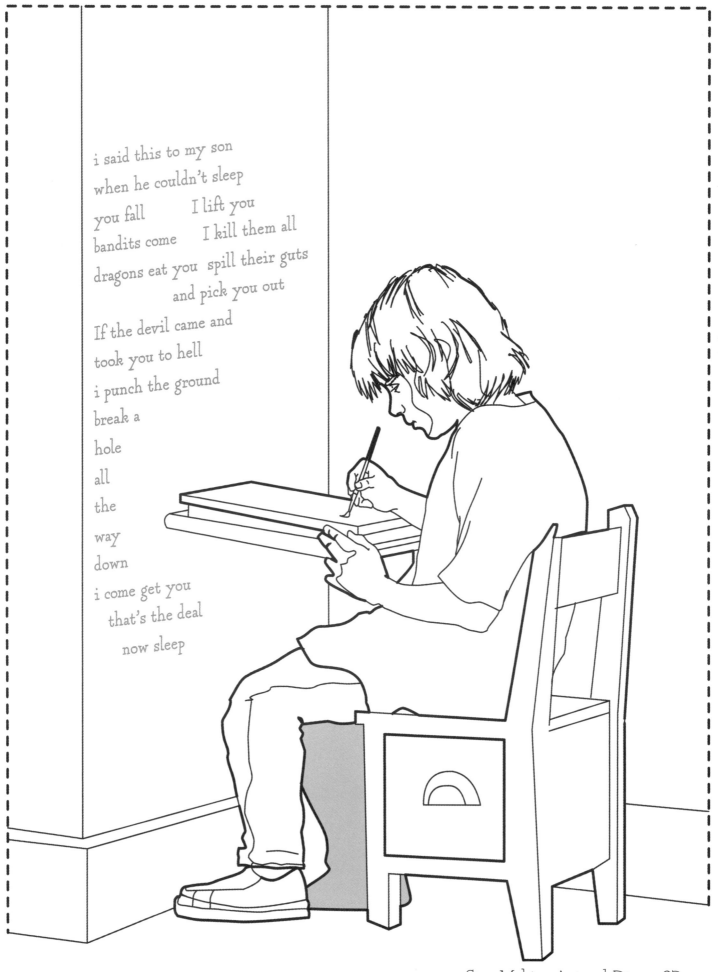

i said this to my son
when he couldn't sleep
you fall   I lift you
bandits come   I kill them all
dragons eat you spill their guts
            and pick you out

If the devil came and
took you to hell
i punch the ground
break a
hole
all
the
way
down
i come get you
    that's the deal
        now sleep

Look at
the space
between
the notes
between
the strokes
between
the beats
between
the lines

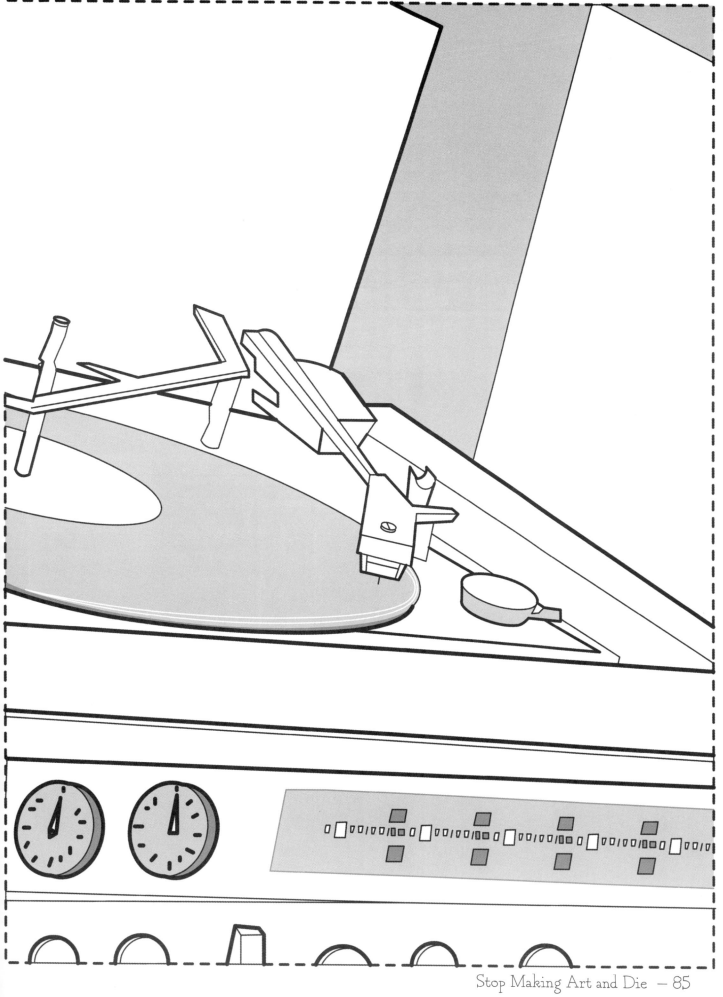

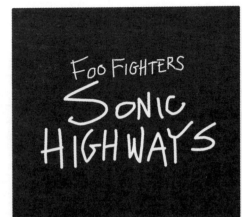

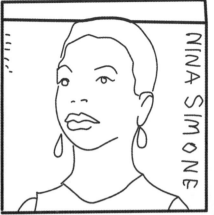

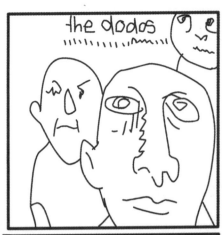

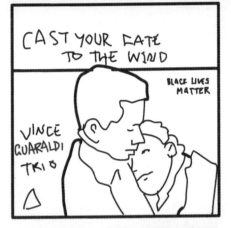

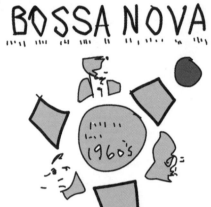

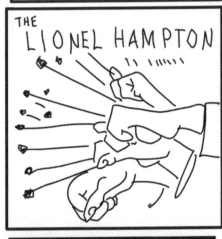

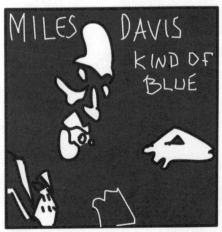

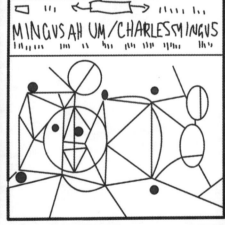

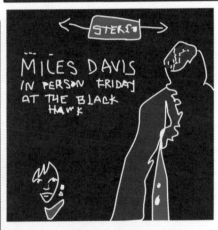

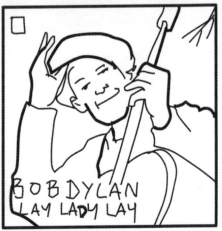

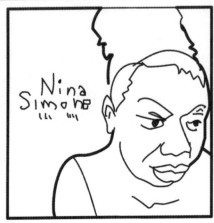

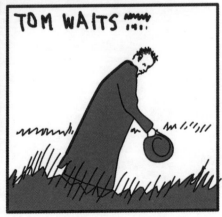

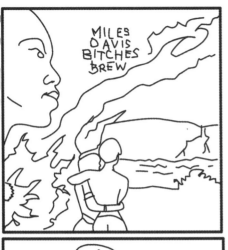

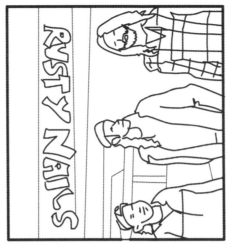

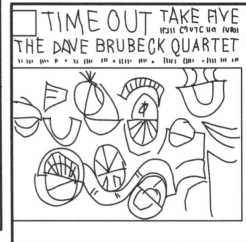

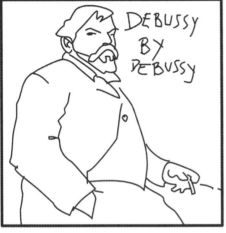

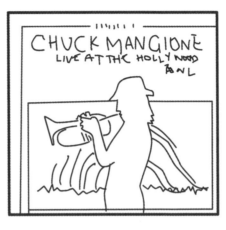

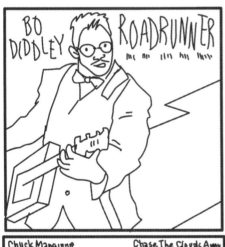

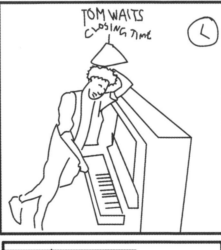

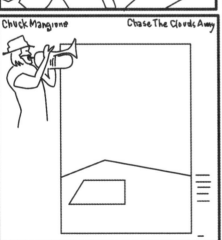

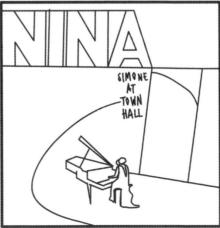

Great music is essential.

I like vinyl records.

You actively engage in listening because every 20 min you have to flip the album.

Listen to the grooves, the gaps between the songs, the space between the beats, the space between the notes.

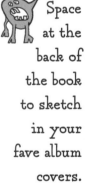
Space at the back of the book to sketch in your fave album covers. Fave book covers too!

Late one night, I had the most vivid dream. I dreamt a Dutchman came into my space while we painted. He didn't speak, he darted around with golden eyes. He wanted to paint with us, but he was too shy. I don't know if I'm telling you Vincent Van Gogh came to me in my sleep or if it was the peanut butter sandwich before bed. It was essential, because that's when I stopped doubting myself.

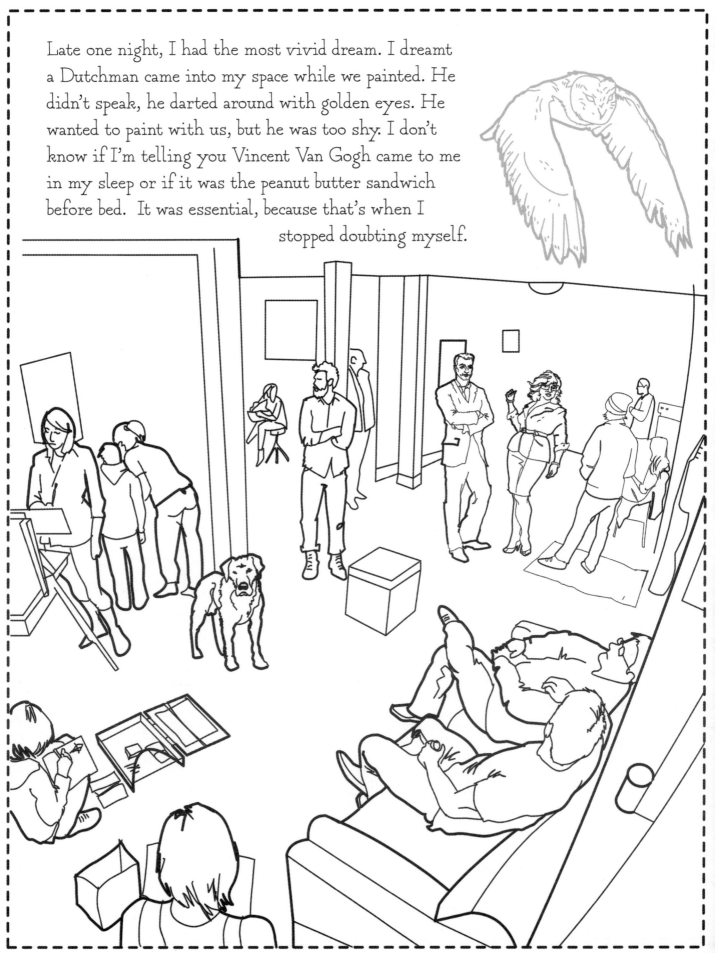

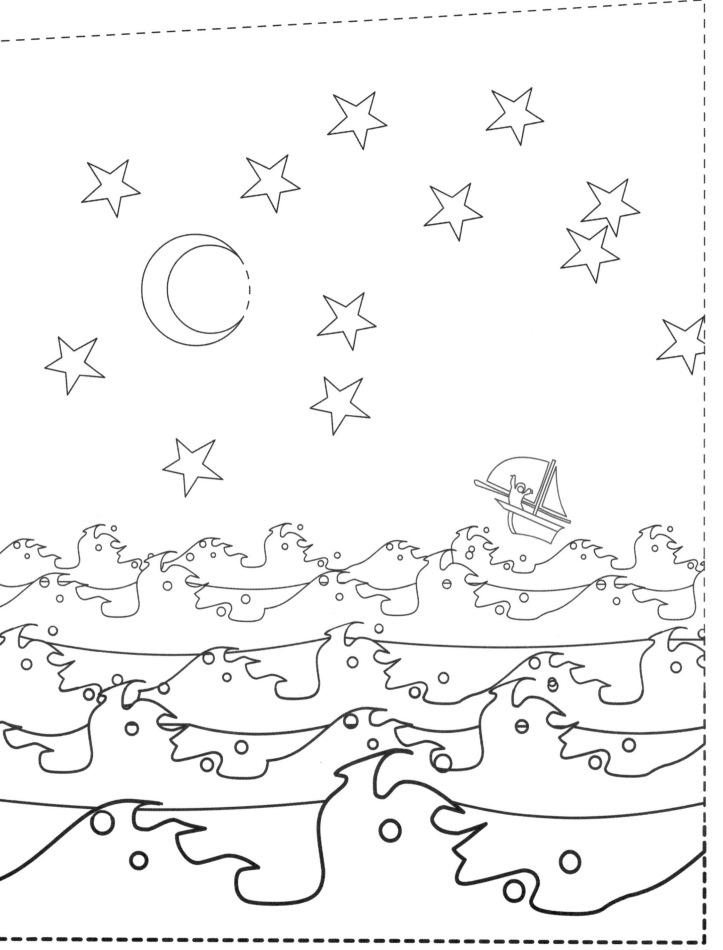

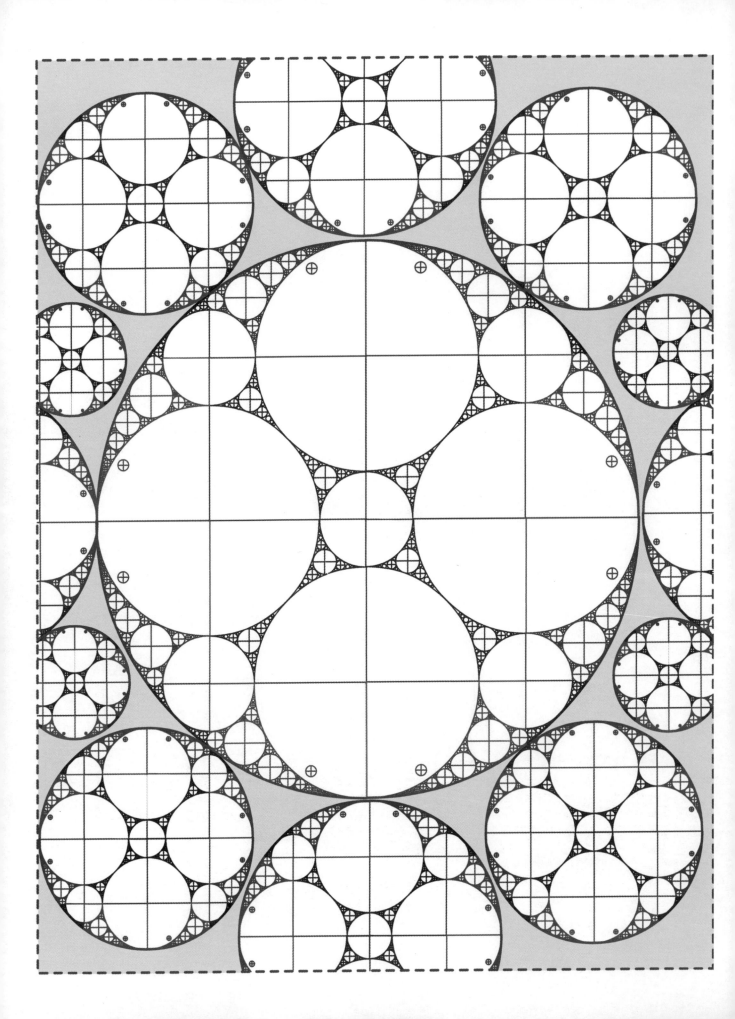

Be happy
half the

time

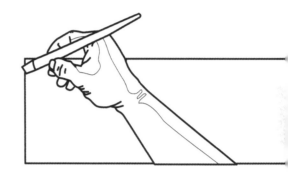

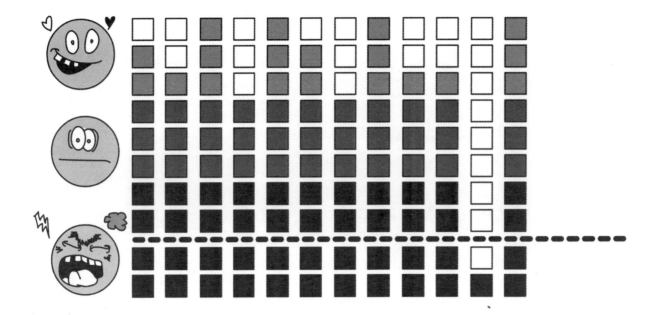

Being happy and feeling happy are two very different things.

We feel pain and joy depending on the extremes of our experiences. If the worst part of a person's life has been getting the wrong tonic water, then not getting the right tonic water is going to hurt as much as a body can manage.

Someone living a much more difficult experience might not even notice drinking the right or wrong tonic water.

Our experiences are relative and our bodies all find a maximum pain and joy in relation to our own extremes.

It seems like you can only feel so much joy, and so many days of joy in a row before you crash.

I've spent most of my life worried about madness.

I know I am not the only one who feels this way.

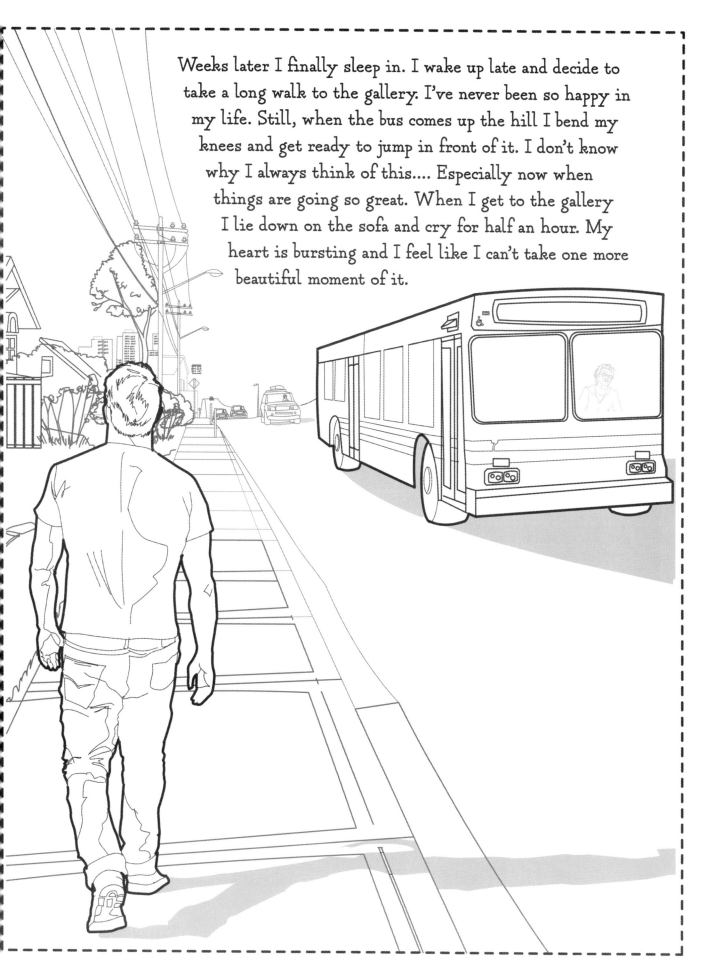

Weeks later I finally sleep in. I wake up late and decide to take a long walk to the gallery. I've never been so happy in my life. Still, when the bus comes up the hill I bend my knees and get ready to jump in front of it. I don't know why I always think of this.... Especially now when things are going so great. When I get to the gallery I lie down on the sofa and cry for half an hour. My heart is bursting and I feel like I can't take one more beautiful moment of it.

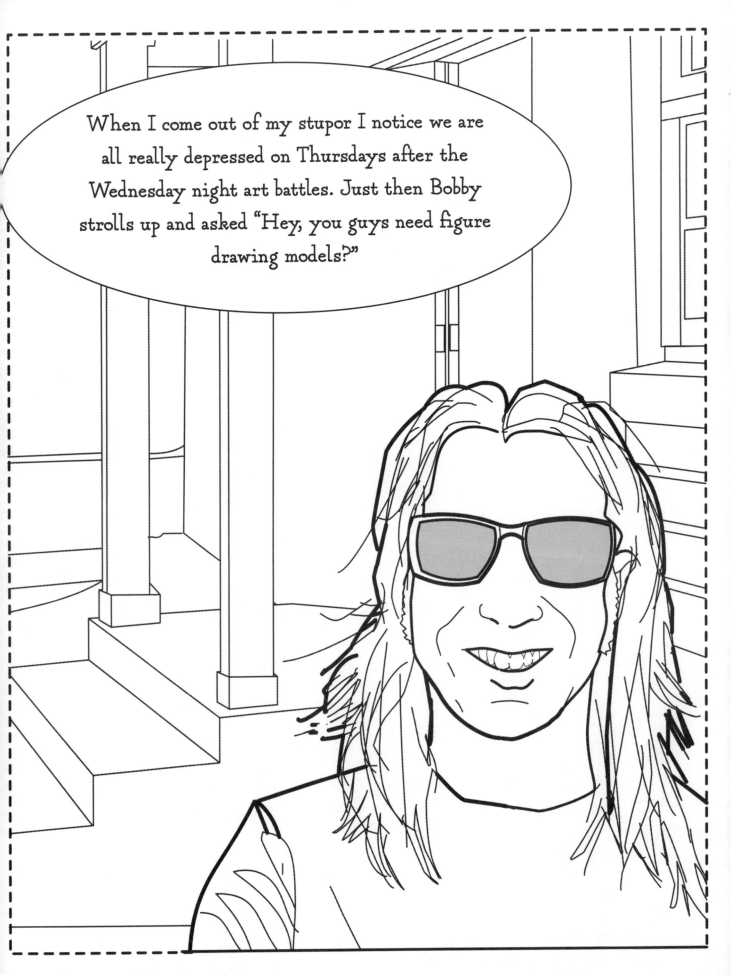

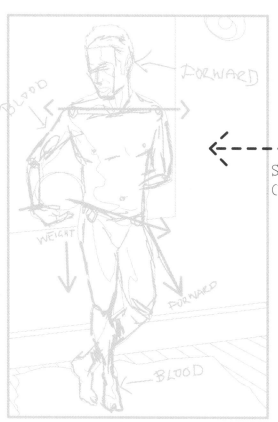

I won't condescend you with a figure drawing lesson. But I'll share this tip. Try using three colours, a light one, a medium one and an intense one.

Start by drawing what you see:
(POSITIVE SPACE)

Then using your mid tone go over top, but this time looking at the space around the model (NEGATIVE SPACE)

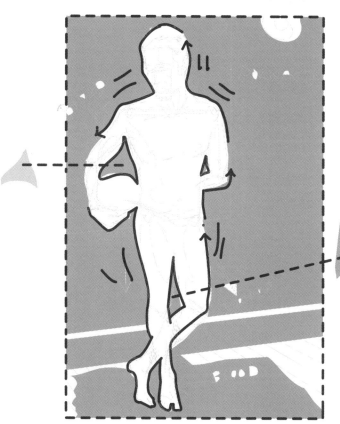

LOOK AT THE SPACE AROUND THE FIGURE

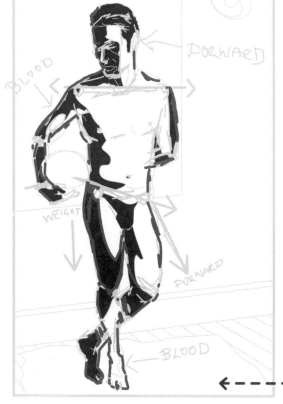

And then go back with your most intense colour and drive right over top correction, adding the shading and the detail.

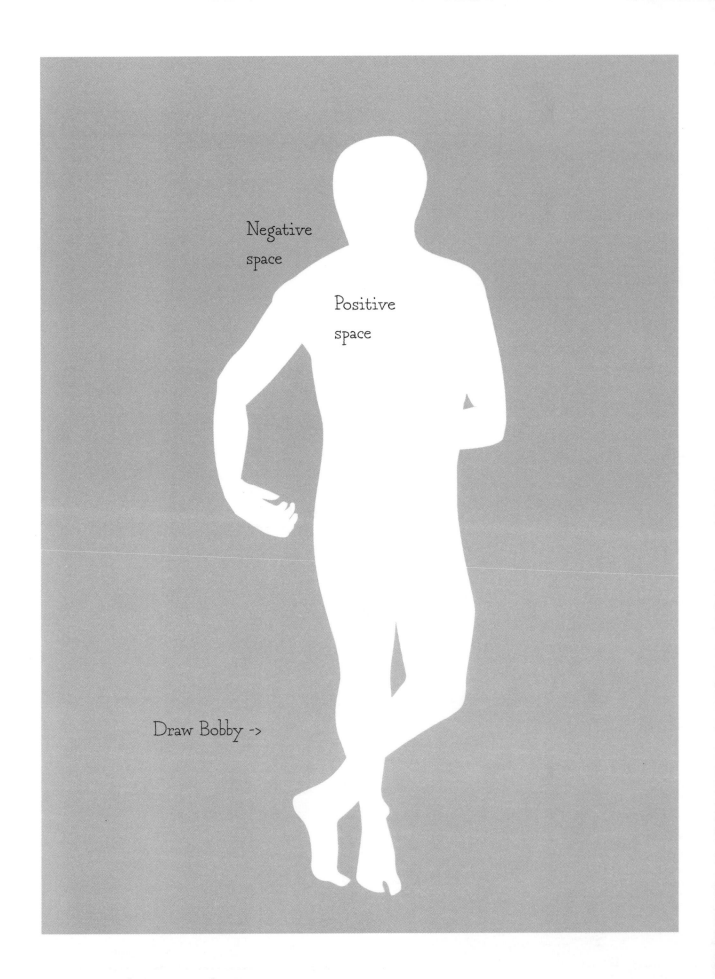

Negative
space

Positive
space

Draw Bobby ->

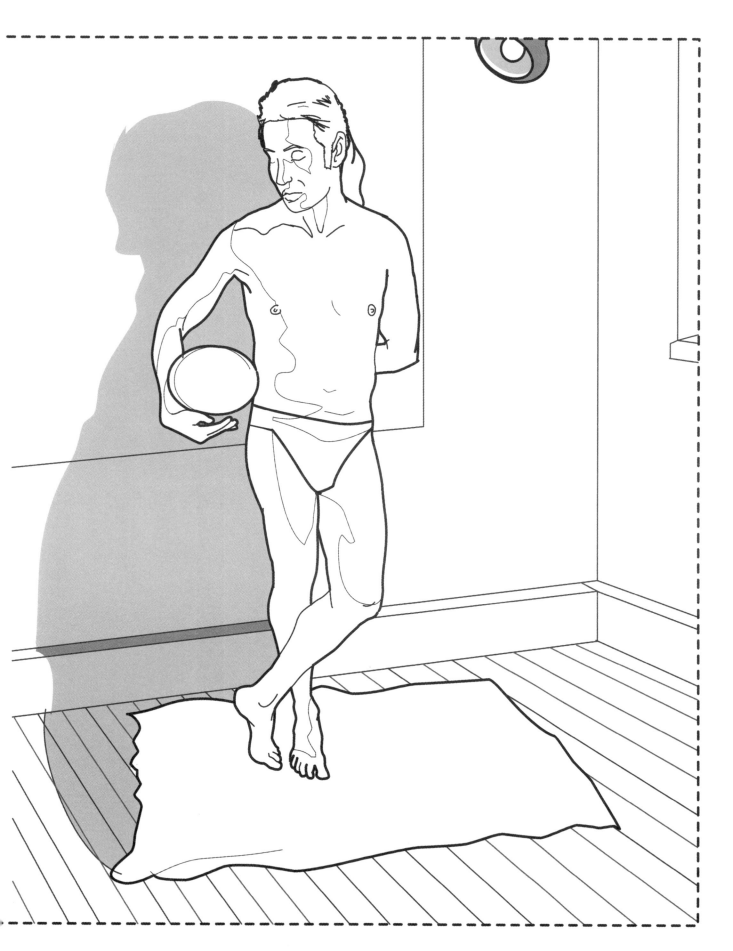

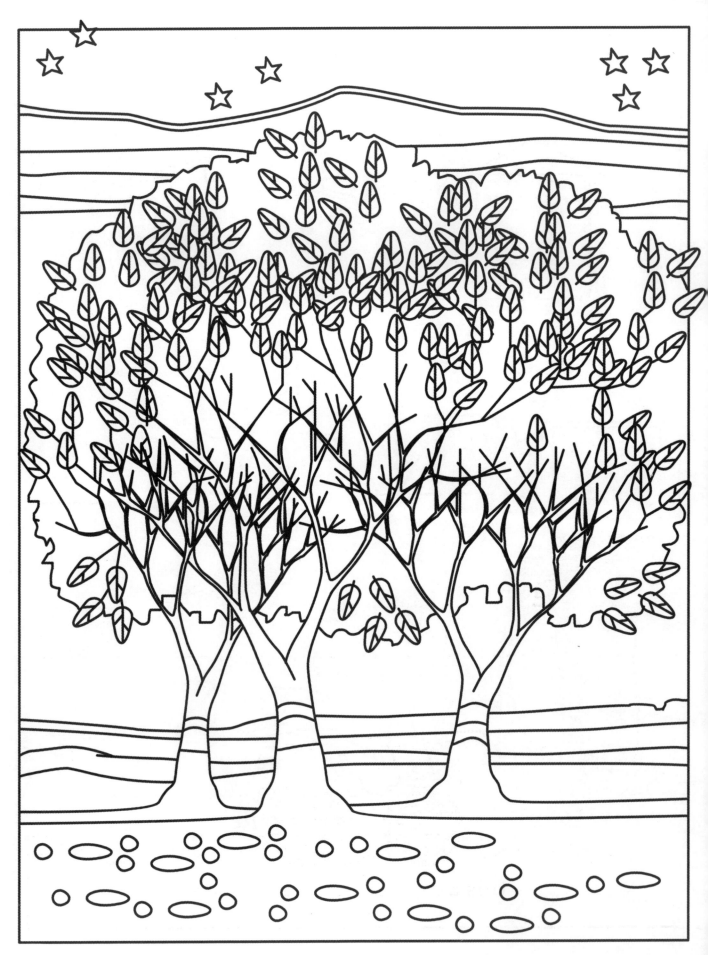

Ever wonder why we do life drawing?

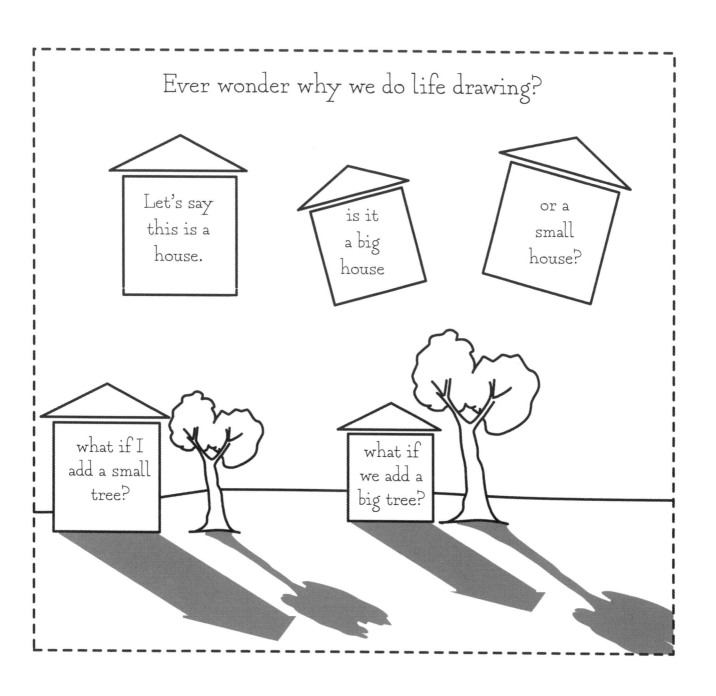

Let's say this is a house.

is it a big house

or a small house?

what if I add a small tree?

what if we add a big tree?

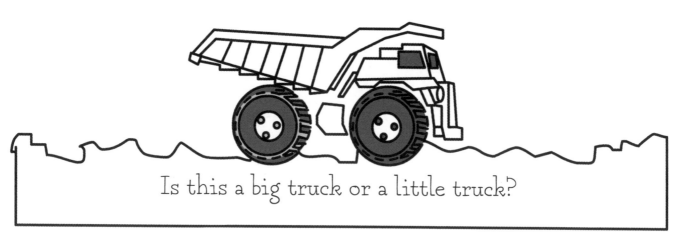

Is this a big truck or a little truck?

We measure out the world in people sizes.

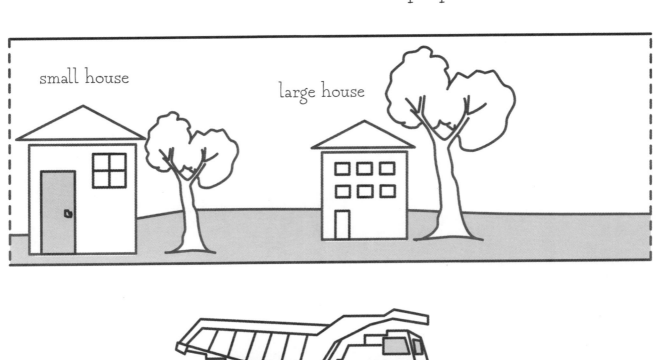

small house

large house

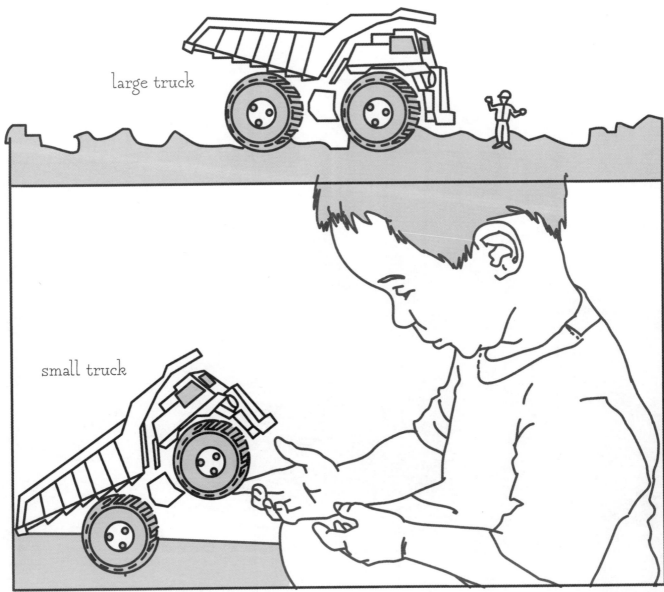

large truck

small truck

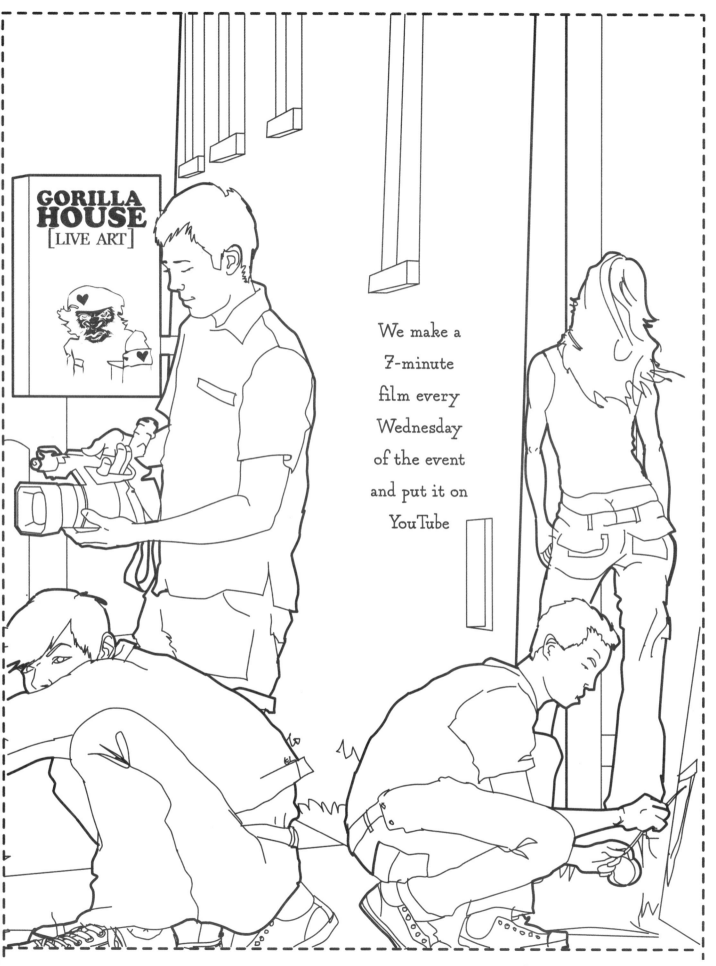

We make a
7-minute
film every
Wednesday
of the event
and put it on
YouTube

We print tiny heart stickers and hand them out at the door when people arrive. The sticker indicates that you have signed a waiver for the video. We print a new heart colour each week and sticker collections flourished.

People around the city start identifying each other by their sticker hearts.

We shoot some short films about our Gorilla House.

The films keep people coming back.

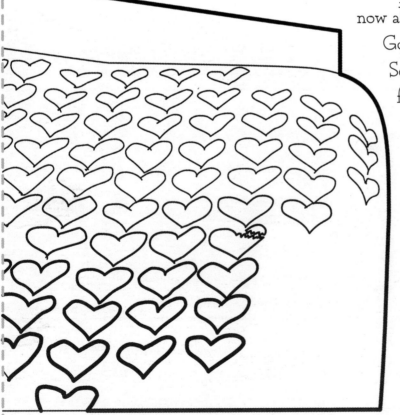

The films keep the thieves away. There's now about 7-hours worth of Gorilla House on the internet, Seeing people drop in and out, fall in love, move away.

It's really beautiful to know those movies are out there.

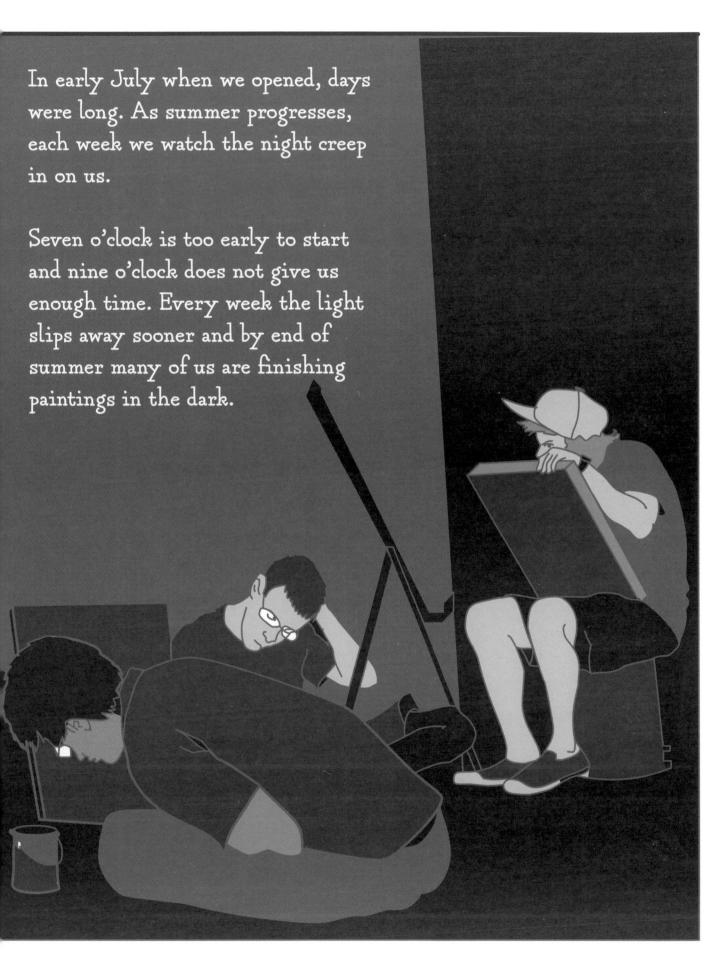

In early July when we opened, days were long. As summer progresses, each week we watch the night creep in on us.

Seven o'clock is too early to start and nine o'clock does not give us enough time. Every week the light slips away sooner and by end of summer many of us are finishing paintings in the dark.

We start holding an event called Gorilla Mouth on
Friday nights where we gather to talk about art.

This is me convincing a room full of
artists that green and purple can make
blue. Someone yells,
"Burn him he's a witch."

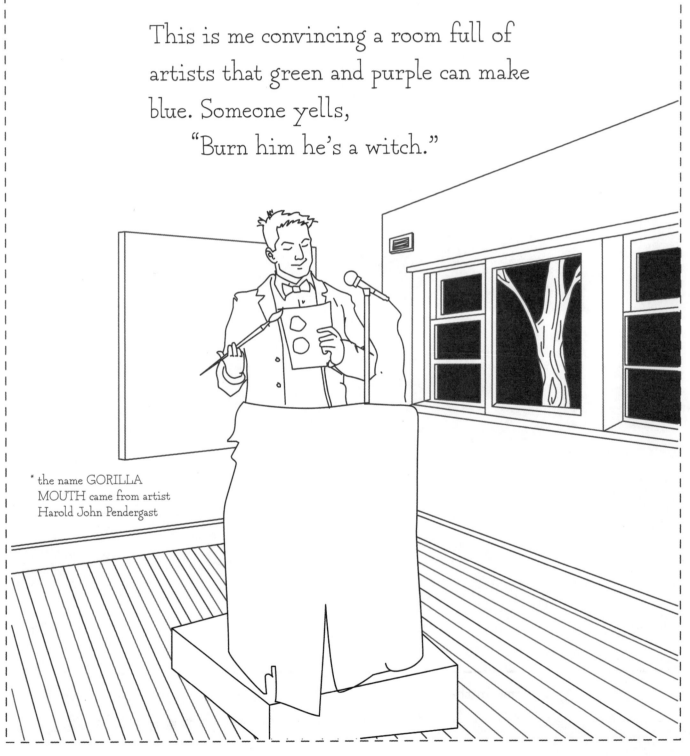

* the name GORILLA
  MOUTH came from artist
  Harold John Pendergast

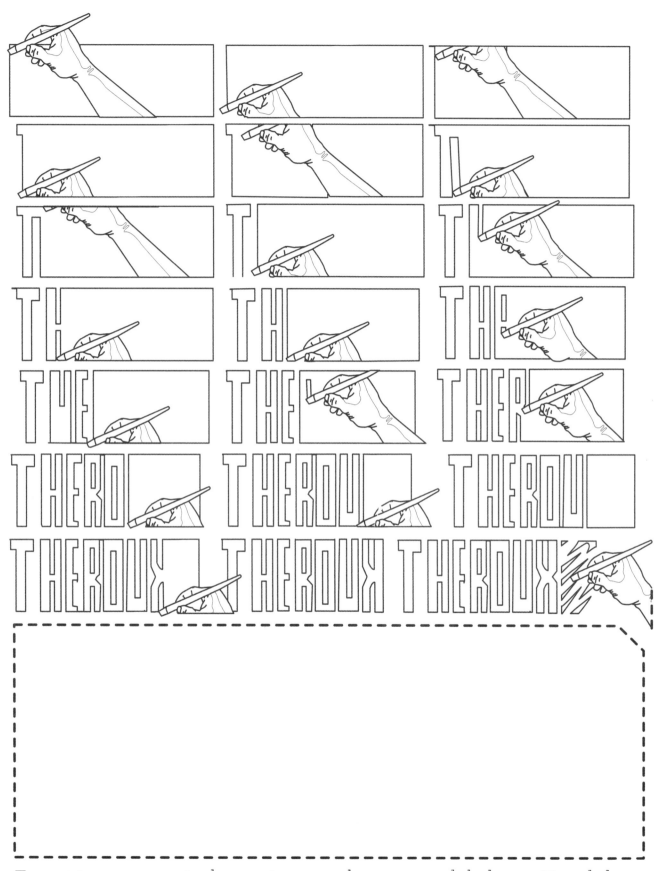

Try writing your name in the negative space, the space around the letters. Use a dark marker and see that your letters remain the white of the page.

Tattoo this tough guy or die.

SURVIVAL ACTIVITIES IX

Bullet
forward

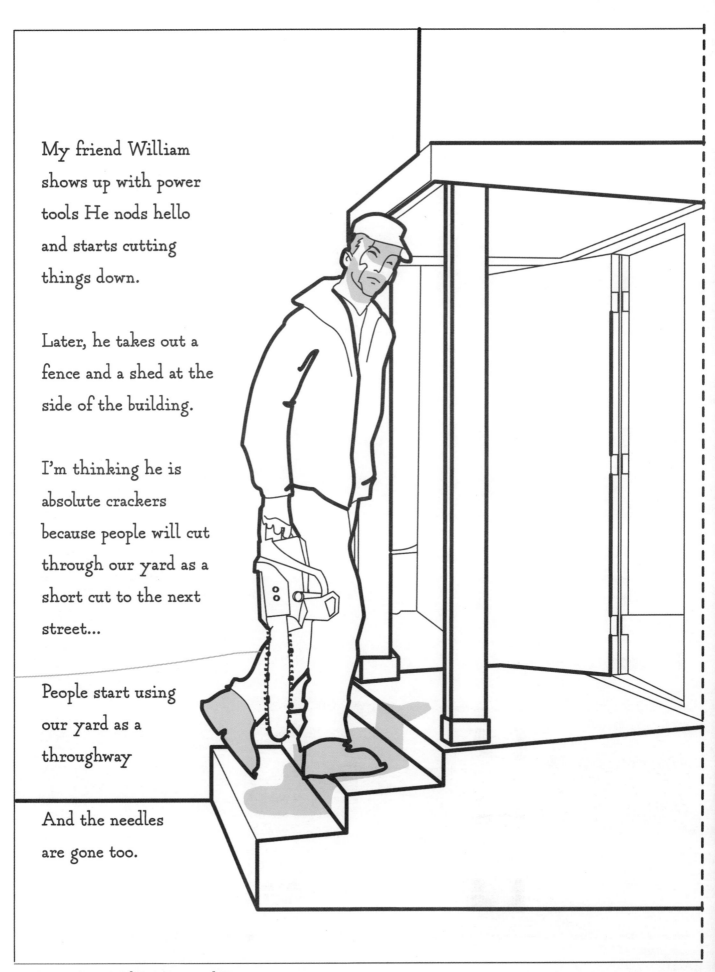

My friend William
shows up with power
tools He nods hello
and starts cutting
things down.

Later, he takes out a
fence and a shed at the
side of the building.

I'm thinking he is
absolute crackers
because people will cut
through our yard as a
short cut to the next
street...

People start using
our yard as a
throughway

And the needles
are gone too.

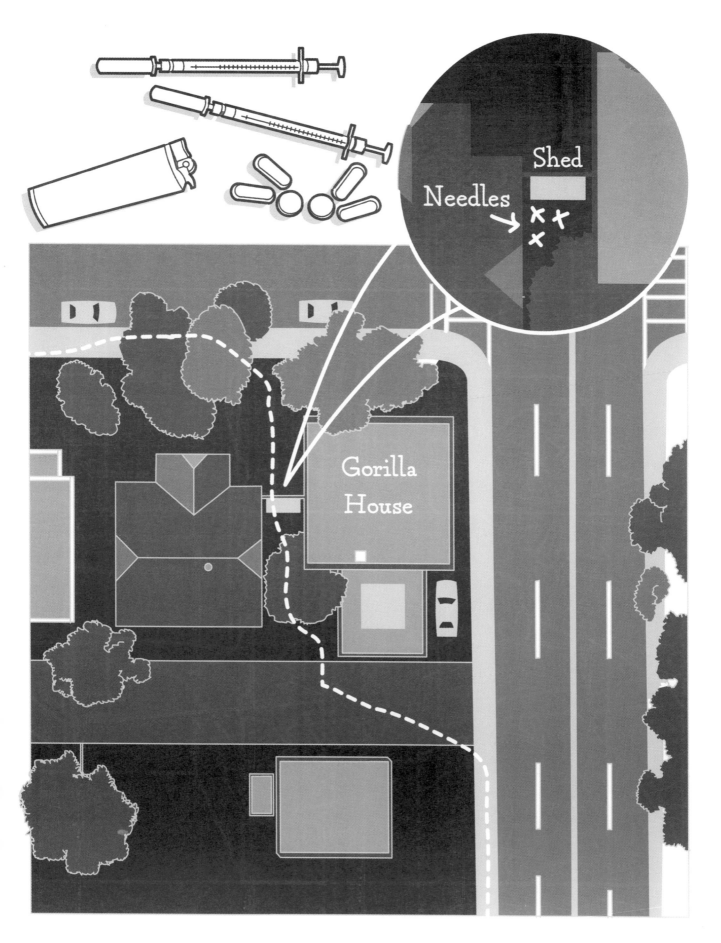

Needles

Shed

Gorilla
House

I'm not here to judge
but I'll tell you this:
Drugs and booze
Drugs and booze give
you brain damage

That's why they seem fun

Drugs and booze don't make
you smarter or more creative

They might make you feel
smarter and more creative

They don't make you more attractive or
the people around you more attractive,
but they might seem more attractive

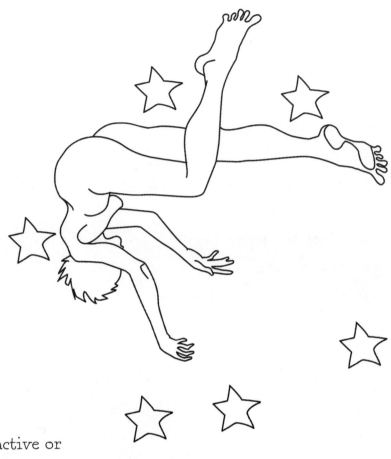

Drugs and booze do not make you or people around you
more interesting, but they might make you feel like the people
around you are more interesting...

Drugs and booze don't sell art
Quality (love) sells art

Drugs and booze are a waste of money and they lead to a much
bigger mess to clean up. Generally.

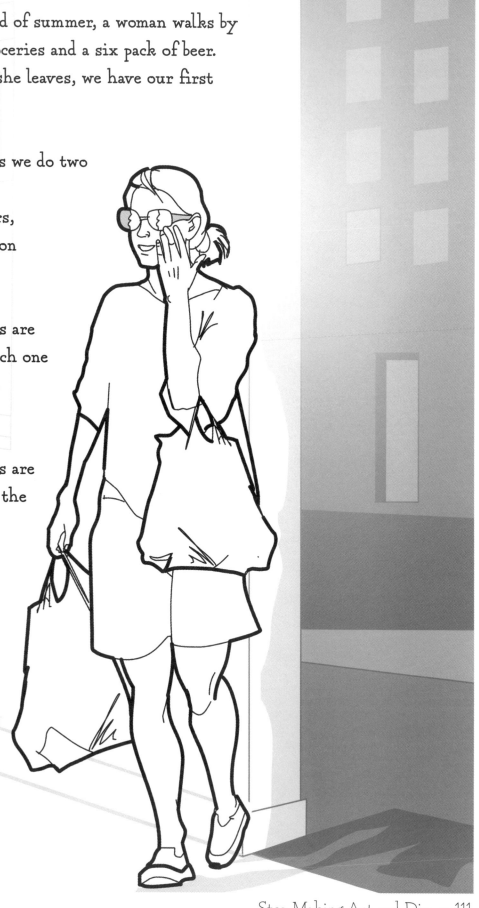

Late one night at the end of summer, a woman walks by the gallery carrying groceries and a six pack of beer. She stops in and before she leaves, we have our first magazine interview.

Over the next few weeks we do two more interviews, for magazines and newspapers, two on TV and a couple on the radio.

All of these news outlets are really supportive, but each one (except live radio) has a lag in broadcast.

None of these interviews are going to be presented to the public until September.

I have every intention of shutting down in September.

I don't want to make fools out of these people who believe in us.

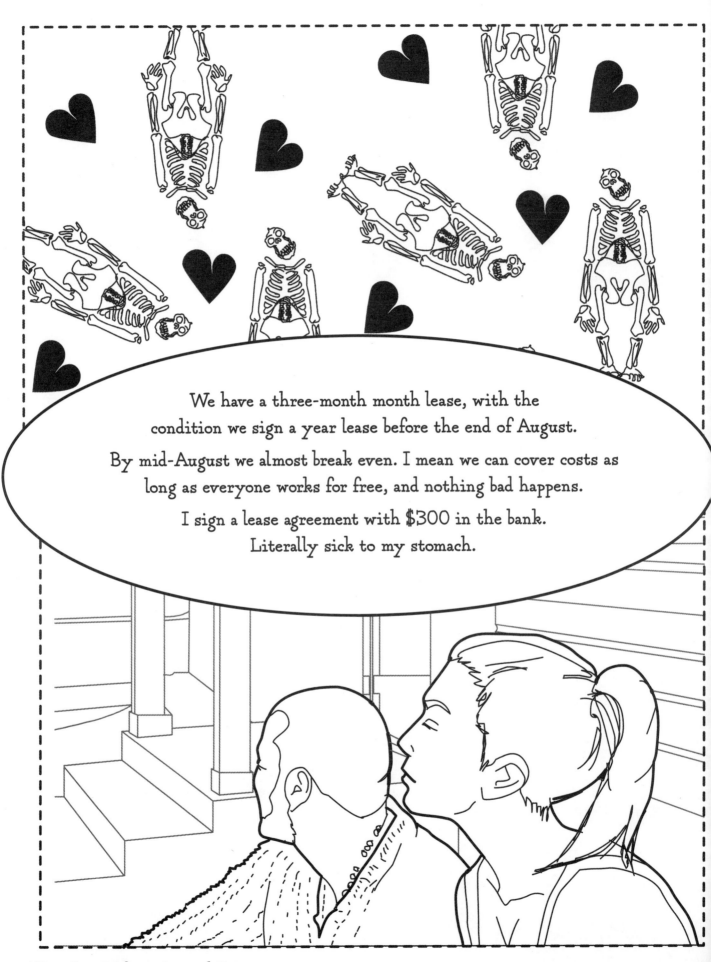

We have a three-month month lease, with the
condition we sign a year lease before the end of August.

By mid-August we almost break even. I mean we can cover costs as
long as everyone works for free, and nothing bad happens.

I sign a lease agreement with $300 in the bank.
Literally sick to my stomach.

Some big things are converging. 1) Gorilla House is really working. I'd expected to lose about $5,000 and by now I've only lost about $4,500. We go from losing $200 a day to losing $25 a day and at this rate I figure in a few months we might even earn some money. 2) I have to go back to school and I figure teaching and running the Gorilla House will kill me (for real). 3) I have a baby on the way. My wife looks at me and says, "Yeah, your Gorilla House is saving us five years of grief," and I say, "Yeah" and we decide I'm moving out after the baby is born. At the same time I worry about the gallery shutting down and getting stuck with the huge rent. Did I mention I have a very real fear of dying from exhaustion? I am also becoming responsible for the wellbeing of a lot of people. Of course I didn't tell anyone the place was only supposed to be open for two months... who in their right mind would want to invest in that?! So here I am, becoming a man all at once.

Then this guy from N.Y. comes in. "DO you know what you have here?" he says. I look around and I see for the first time what we've built.

Just like that, I'm back teaching school. I'd opened an art gallery and worked about six hundred hours over the summer instead of resting. I feel pretty strong and I am actually glad to be back. I tell my new principal that I accidentally opened an art gallery, that I plan to work until at least 4:30 every day and if it ever seems like I'm not getting my job done to let me know. She is pretty nice about it.

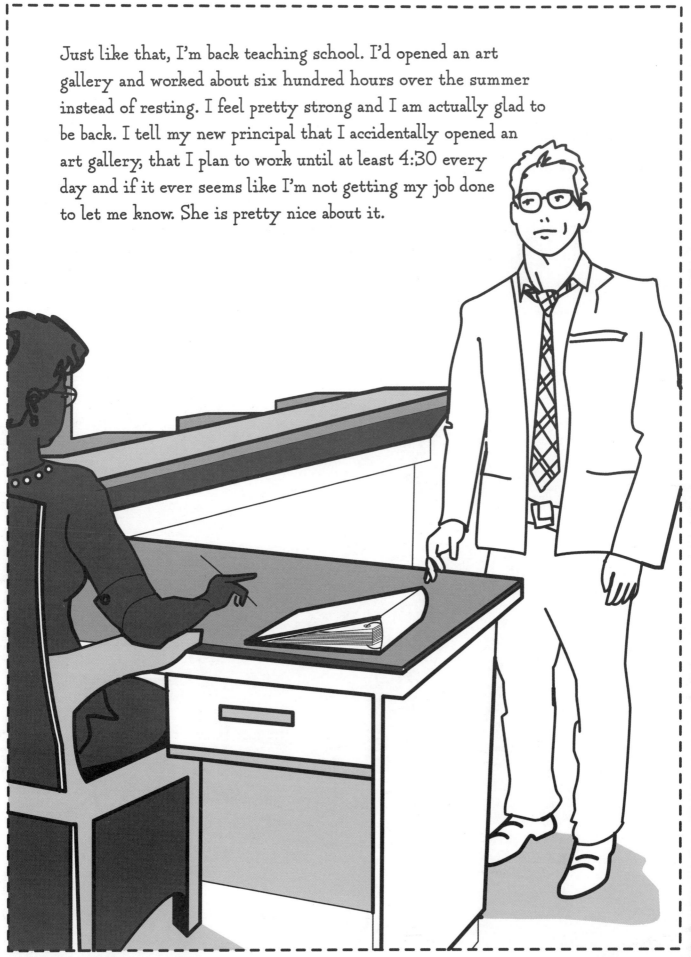

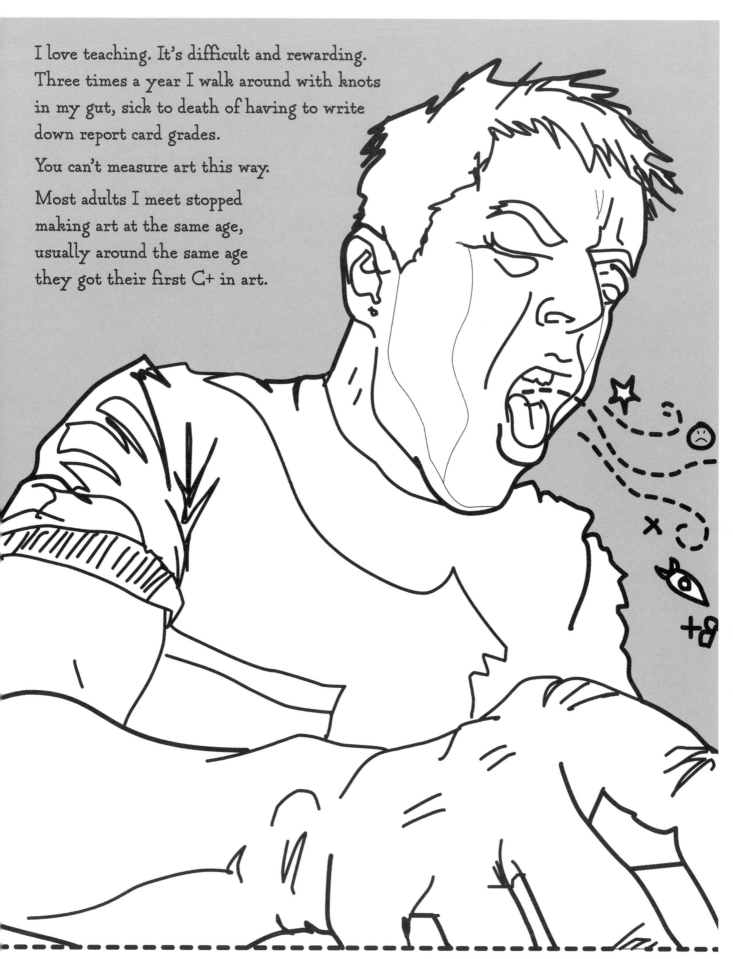

I love teaching. It's difficult and rewarding. Three times a year I walk around with knots in my gut, sick to death of having to write down report card grades.

You can't measure art this way.

Most adults I meet stopped making art at the same age, usually around the same age they got their first C+ in art.

The next few
months are a blur.

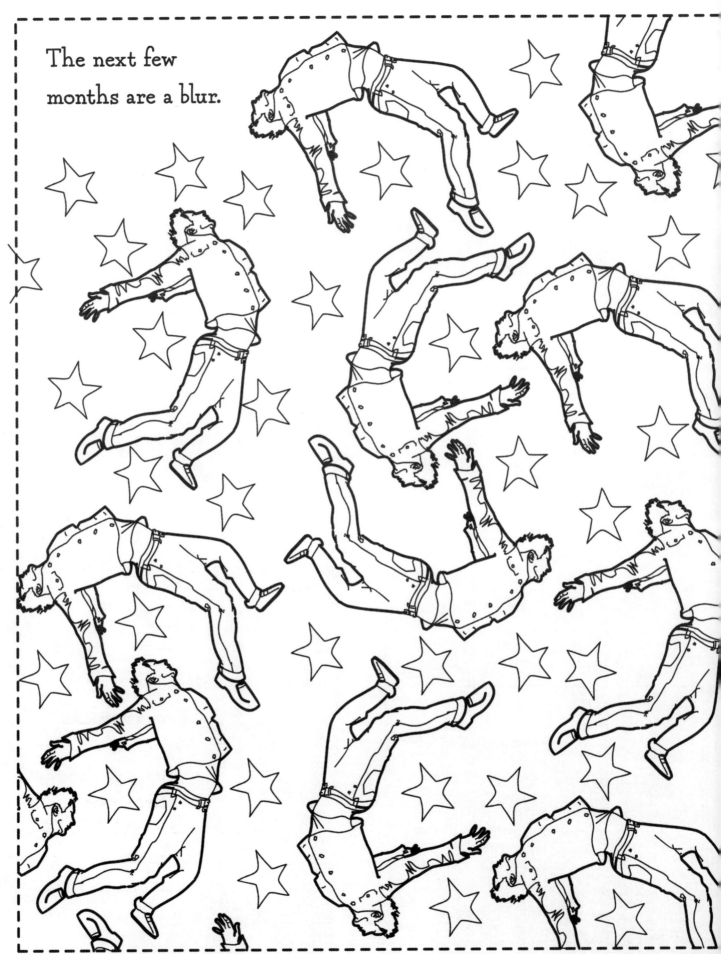

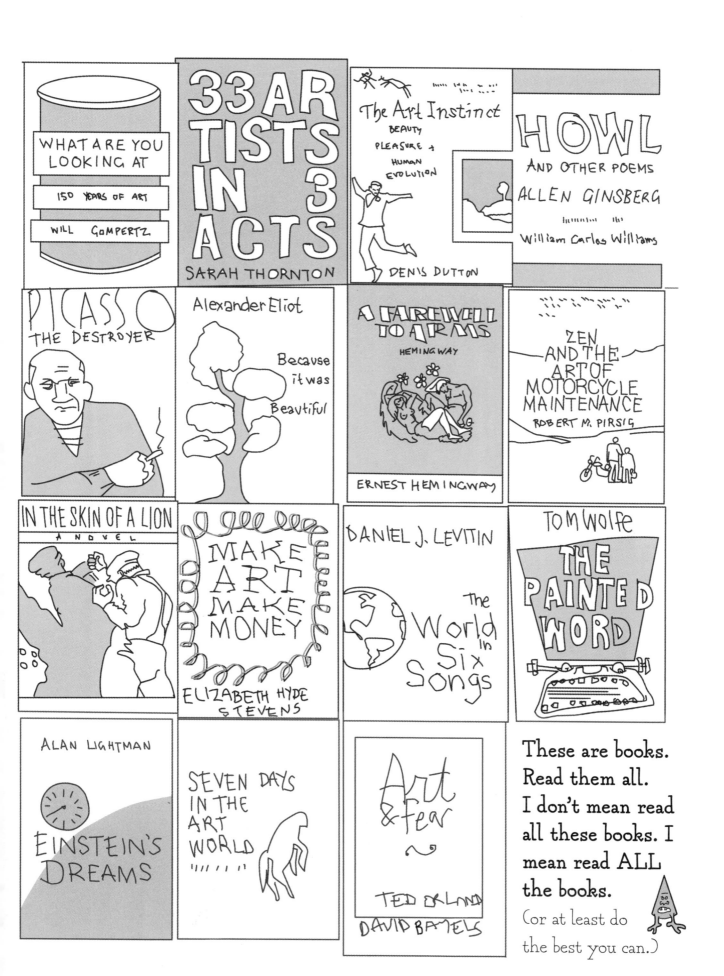

These are books. Read them all. I don't mean read all these books. I mean read ALL the books. (or at least do the best you can.)

Do you want to know
how to tile?

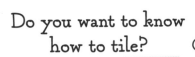

Cut in half

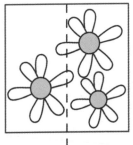

First draw some stuff

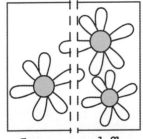

Separate and flip

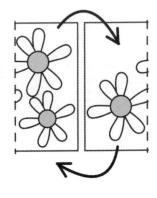

Tape

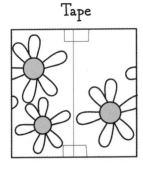

And draw some more

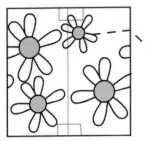

Cut again

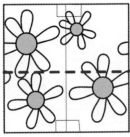

Separate again

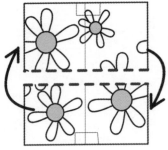

Tape

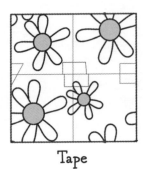

And draw over
the edges

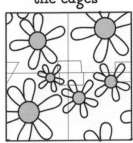

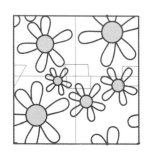

You can copy
as many as
you like, on
the computer
or with a
photocopier.
Put them
together and
all the edges
will match up,
on to infinity

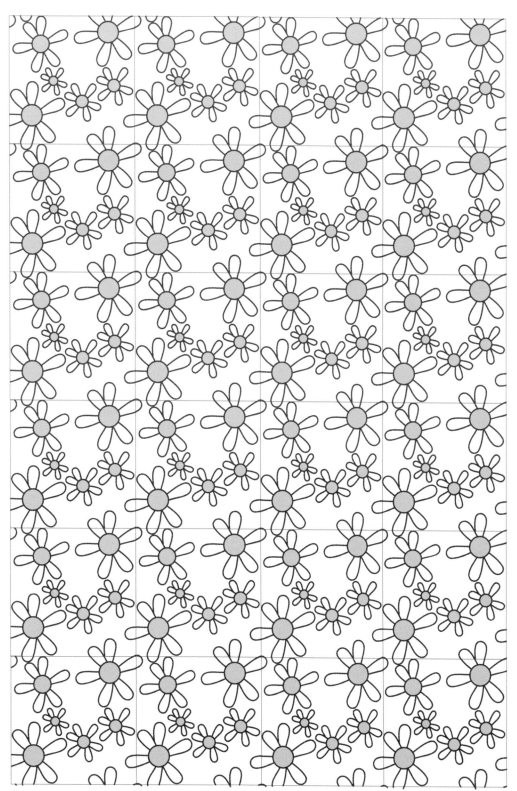

After being open for three months, the first hotdog guy shows up.

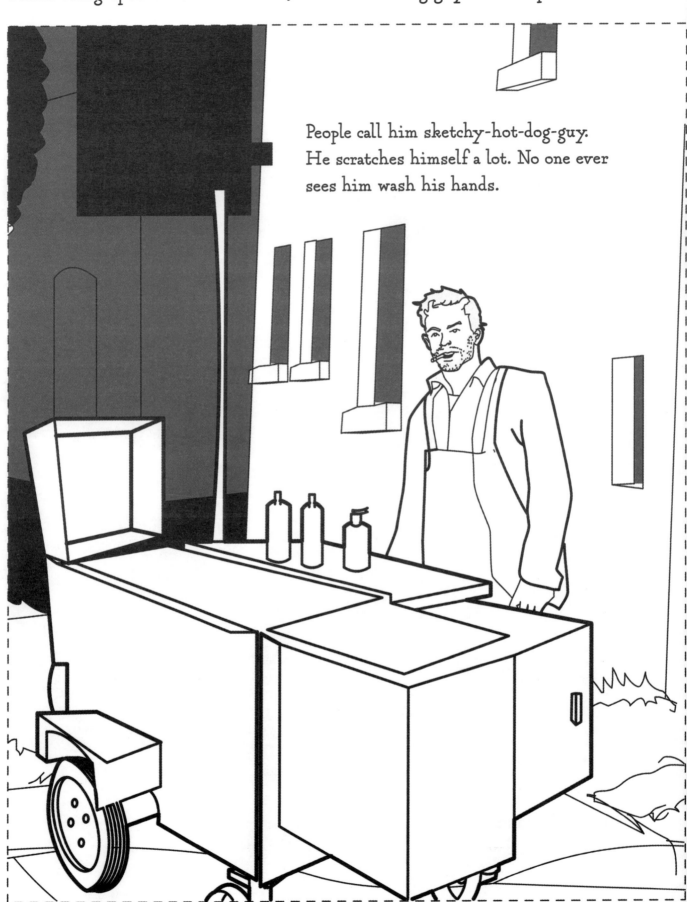

People call him sketchy-hot-dog-guy.
He scratches himself a lot. No one ever
sees him wash his hands.

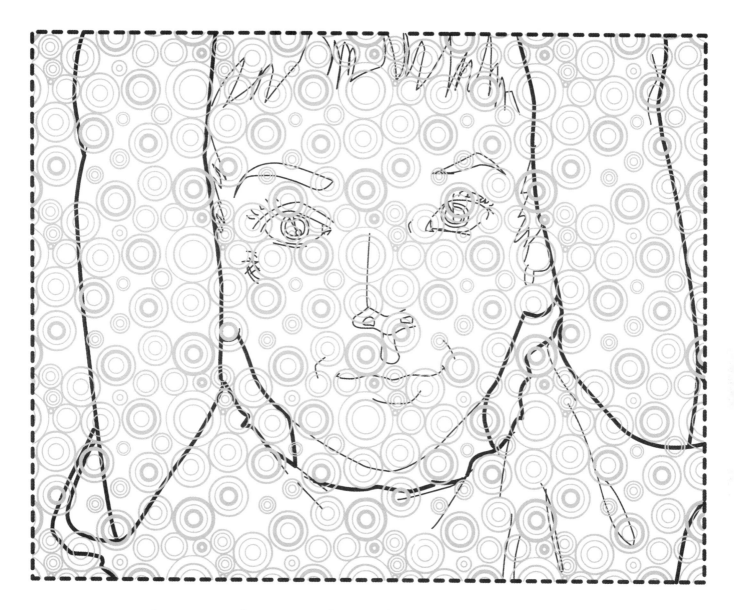

Late one night we start hanging a show and everyone is in a bad mood. We look for an excuse to quit, or delay, or postpone. William walks into the studio and tells us that Ryan died.

Everyone starts crying. I am confused, the only Ryan I know is a 7 years old. Everyone knows 7-year-olds don't die. 71-year-olds die.

I start crying too. We walk over to see if there is anything we can do for his mom but she isn't home. Two cop cars are outside.

Ryan and his mom were two free spirits and part of our family. Ryan's spirit broke free that day. We all cried and then we keep hanging the show.

We carry on. In my heart I am kind of ashamed we are able to carry on.
I wonder if we are doing the right thing.
Like, when a drummer dies and the whole rock band calls it quits.
A few weeks later like a ghost, Ryan's mom floats in.
She'd lost her son and she floats in like a grey sheet.
And I try to say I'm sorry but she won't hear it.
She says, "Well, stupid... I'm here now."

And then I know carrying on was the thing to do.
And we carry on no matter what.

One night while I'm editing a film I overhear a woman's voice say from the back room, "...Oh, I just feel like, when I put my work in a real gallery I just feel..." I stop my work. Then she says, "I just rather hang in a a real art gallery, it's so much nicer and then I feel..."

I think if it was a man's voice, I'd go in the other room and chuck him out the front door, but I sit there and burn, frozen with rage.

Finally I ask Elijah if he'd heard what I heard.
He says matter-of-factly, "The last show she hung was in a laundromat."

So it's pretty cool I didn't go screaming my head off at her because she meant she was actually happy to be in a
REAL ART GALLERY.

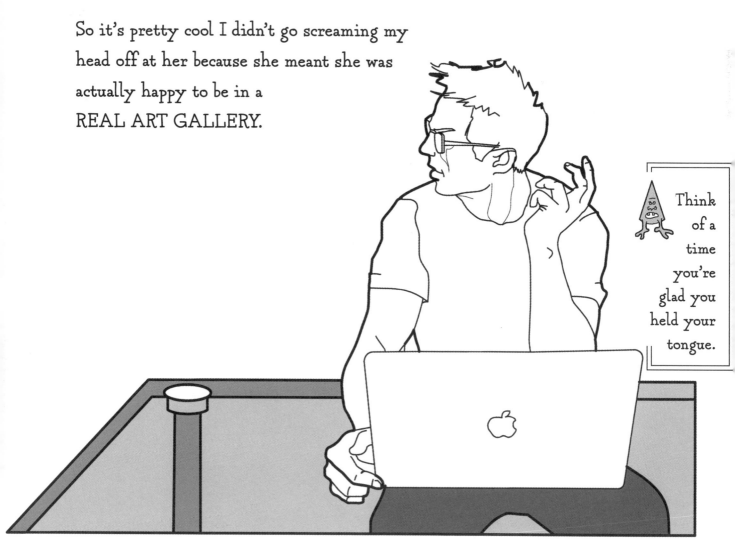

Think of a time you're glad you held your tongue.

Some days are incredibly difficult.
Draw in some background or die.

Some days are rough.
Draw in some background or die.

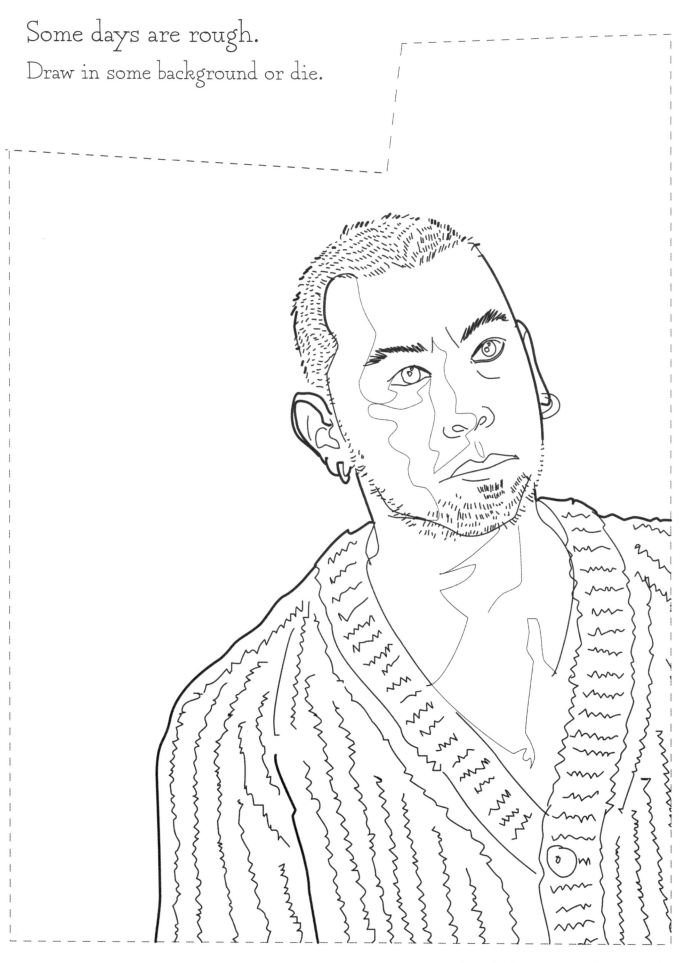

Some days are just awesome.
Draw sweetness and light background or die.

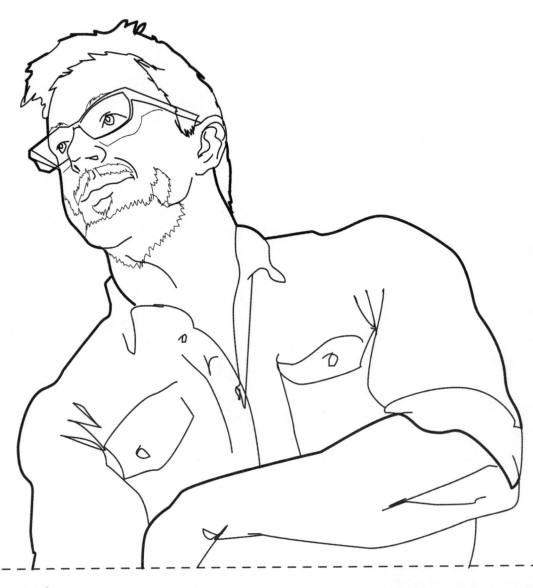

... and there is this girl

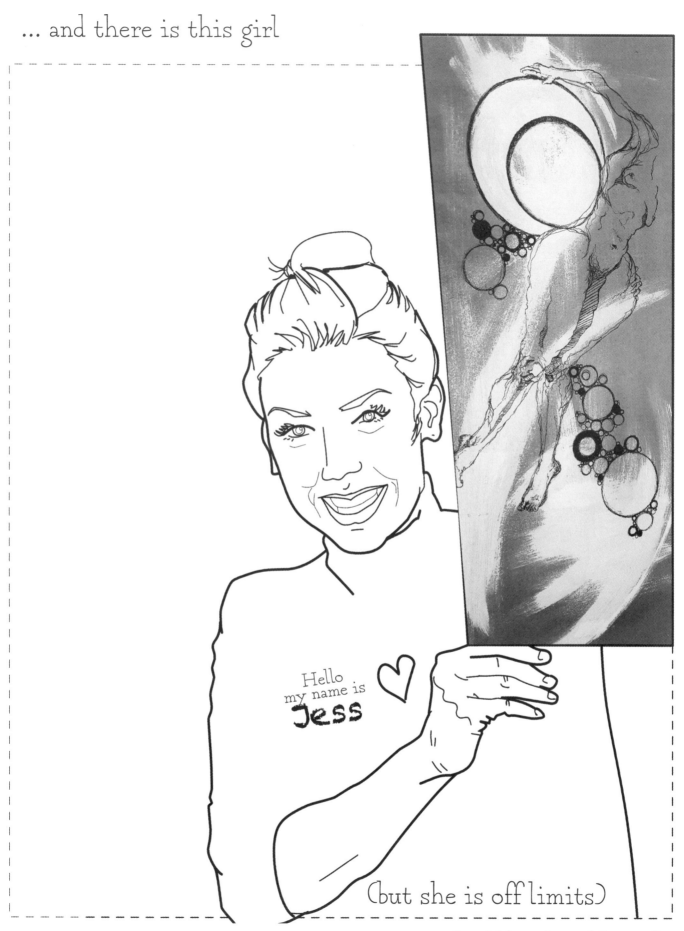

Hello
my name is
Jess

(but she is off limits)

One night a couple of big guns arrive.

We never miss a Wednesday.

Draw holiday decorations or die.

Even if it is Christmas Eve

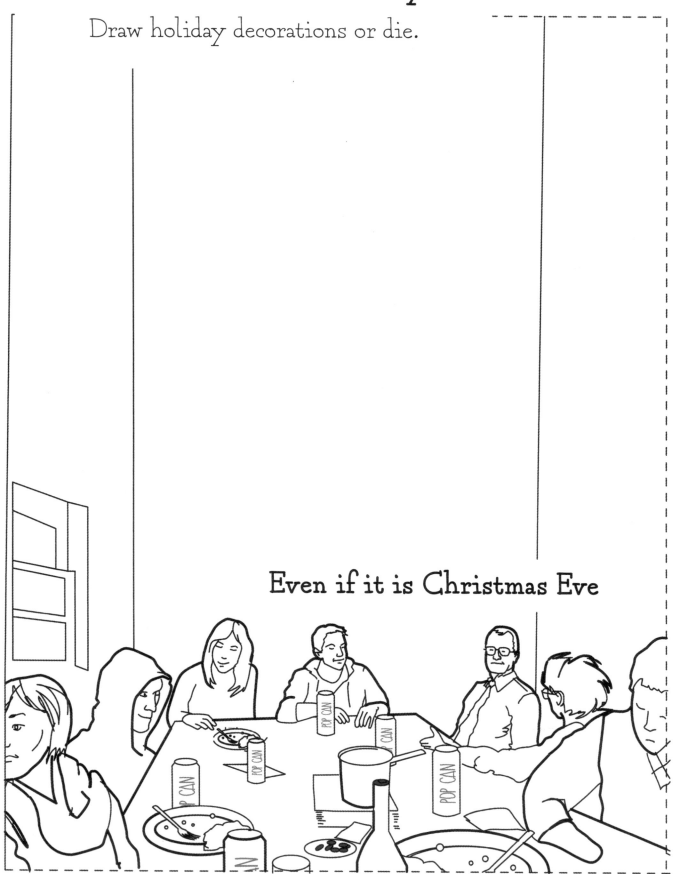

In the next activity section, some trees get uprooted in the flood so here I am, thinking about them early. Have you ever tried to draw a tree and found it looked like it was stacked together out of wood?

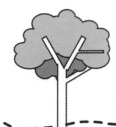

It's easy if you draw them the way they grow.

Roots grow this same way too.

You draw a line for the trunk and split it in half, each branch splits in half at the end, if you like math, the size of each branch is a 1:1.16 ratio to the branch that came before.

Start with a seed
They split into 2
And split into 2

(Grow these seeds into trees)

Hearts
flooding
with joy

It starts to rain.

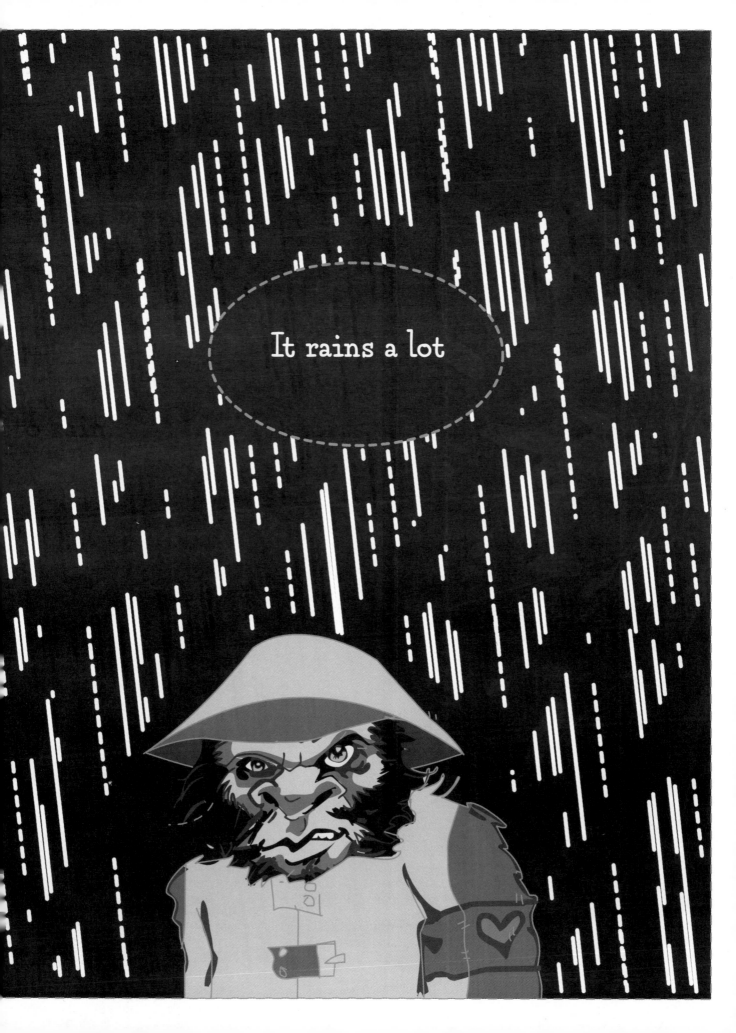

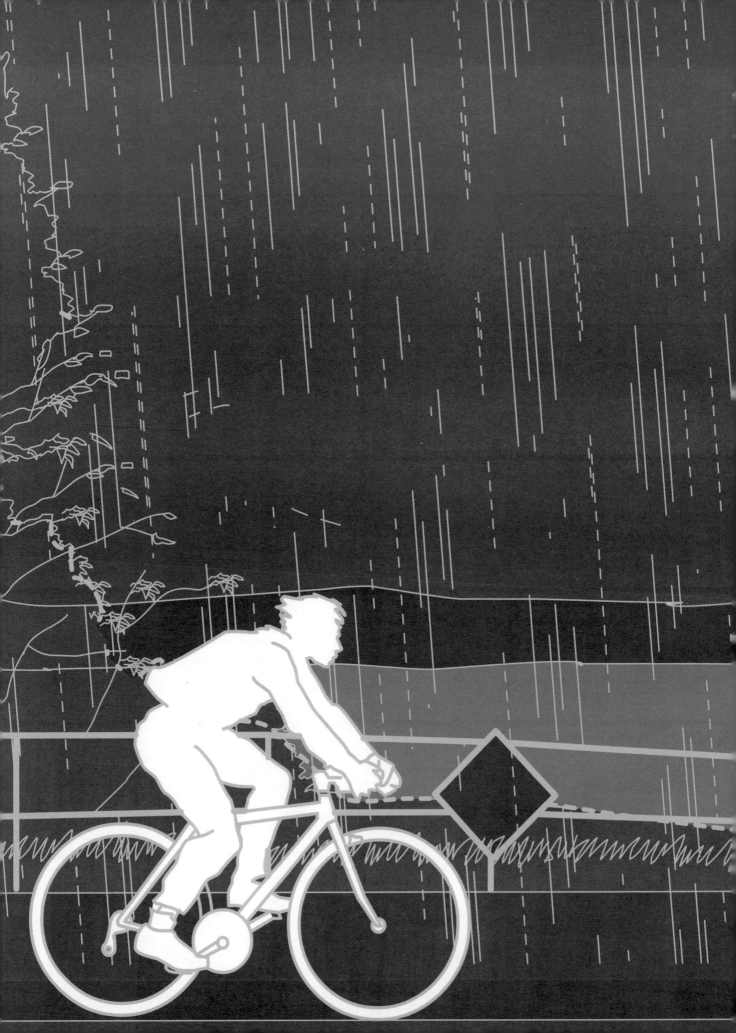

The city gets evacuated.
I decide to ride my bike home.
Am I surrounded by thunder?
It isn't thunder, it is the sound of
trees being snapped off and carried
away by the river.

For the next few days the city is shut down. Cops and rescue workers are up three days straight. Some gorillas and I get on our bikes, with bike baskets full of coffee.

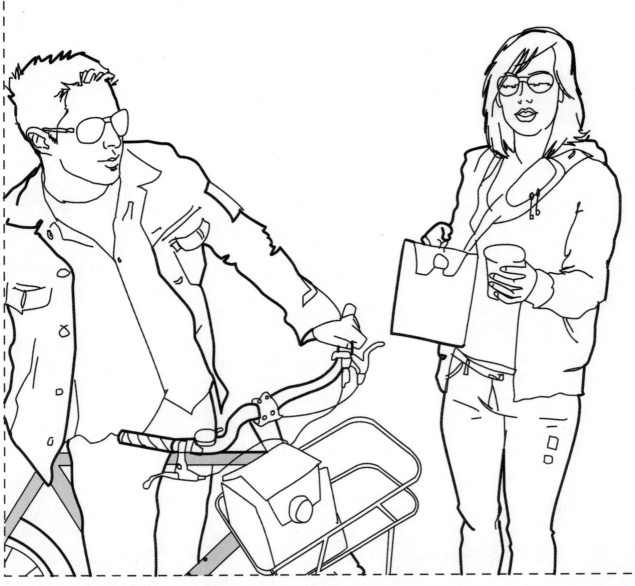

Some cops reach for their guns, as we step over the line but
they are all
grateful for the coffee.

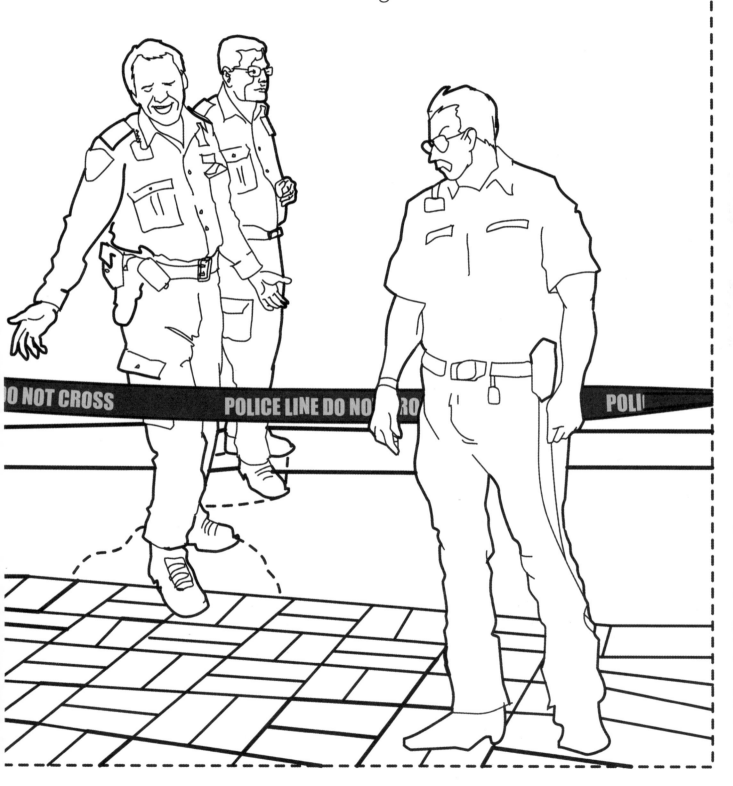

This could be the end.

But people keep coming. And the auctions are abysmal. But people keep coming. And where before, people used to complain that they hadn't sold their work for enough money...

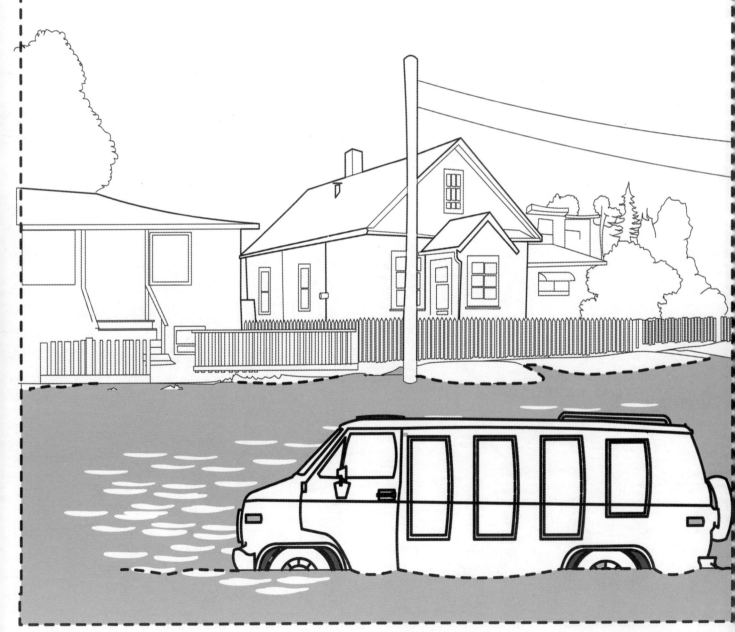

...now there is no money, and strangely, no more complaints.

I guess people are looking to Gorilla House for some normalcy.

Well, then things get pretty strange.

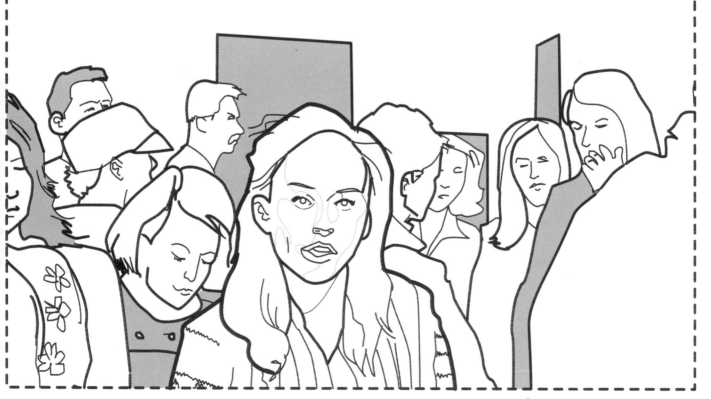

We have a handshake deal with the landlord for when the Gorilla House lease runs out. Not long after it runs out, the upstairs tenants move out. I suggest that we would be happy to take over the upstairs space if he can't find a tenant. The landlord says he'll let us know.

We've had a rule up until this point. The first week we moved in, Elijah laid down a strip of tape and said, "we never clean past this point, if we do, we lose the building."

We clean past that point.

The landlord.
sells the building.
and tells us
        we have to move out.

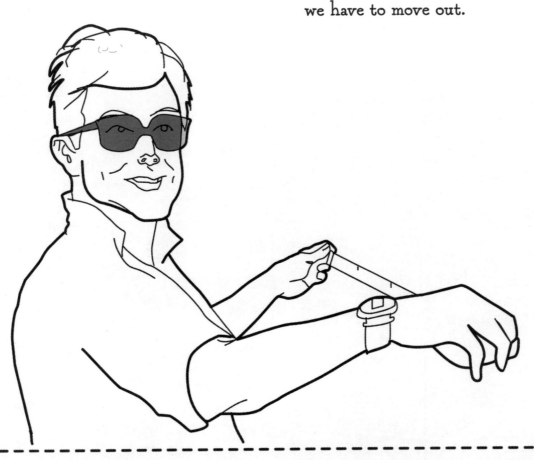

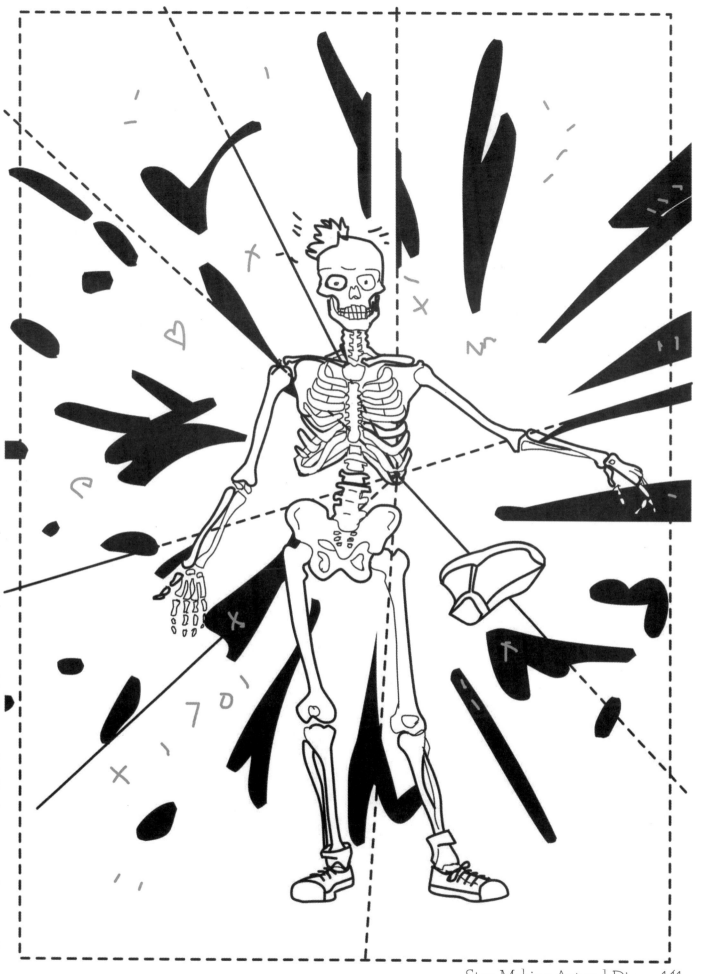

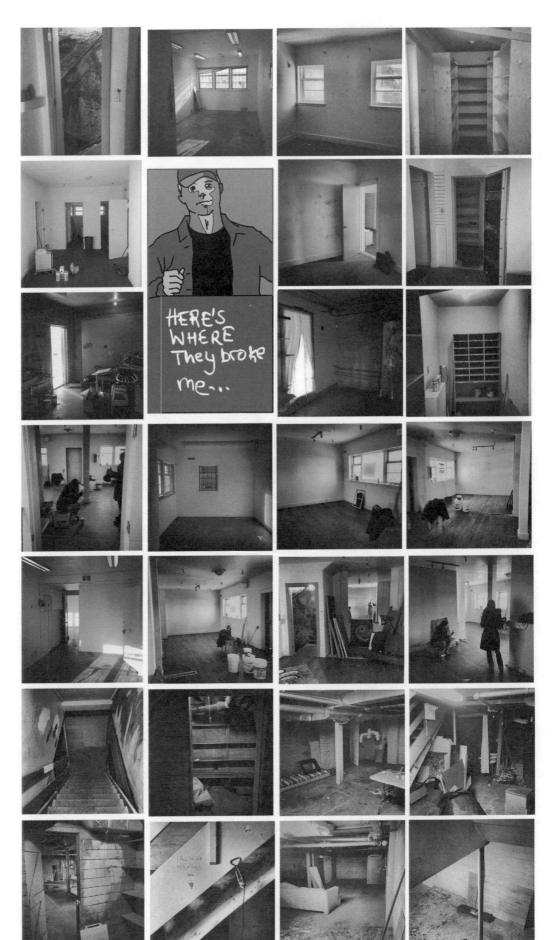

"This is where I fell in love with myself."

(Rebecca Sulley)

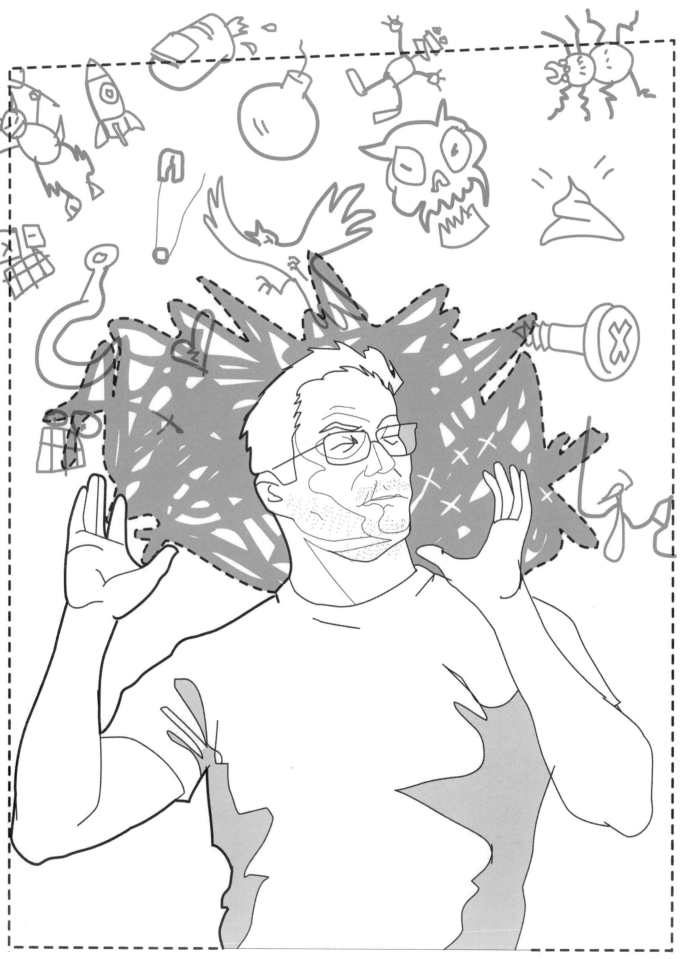

We clean out Gorilla House for 14 days and 14 nights, taking breaks on Christmas Eve to host our orphan's dinner and then again on New Years Eve.

We clean until late Sunday night, until right before we go back to school.

At first there were ten of us, then five. By the last few days there are only two of us.

My ex-wife calls. She asks, "How are you doing?"

I say that I am doing fine. She said, "Who's there helping you?" I say it is just Jessica.

She says, "You are an idiot, you'd better ask her out. If she'll still have you."

So I do. And I guess closing down doesn't seem so bad.

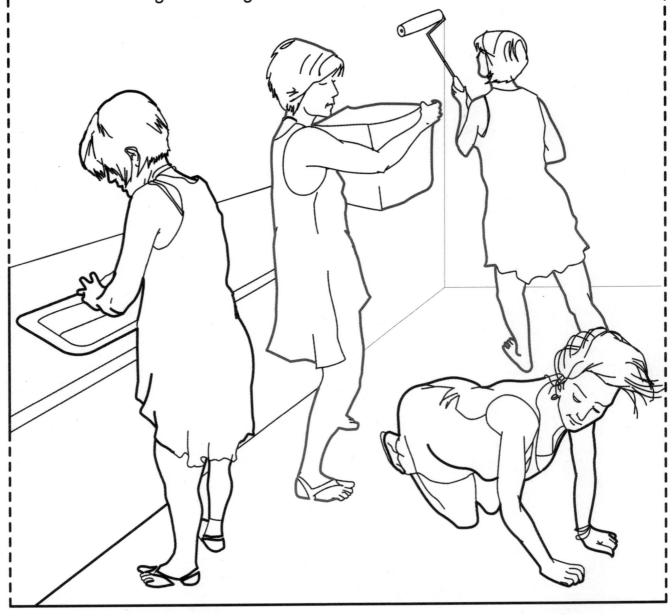

SURVIVAL ACTIVITIES XI

Wedge
between

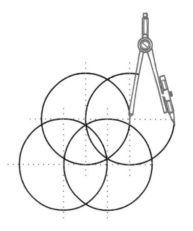

Dear Rich

Get up and fight

there will be

an army

behind you

There's more beauty

than ugly

there's more kindness

than greed

there's more hope

than sallow

Be the wedge

between the thesis

and the antithesis

make room to

make change

and if you fail

make sure you

go down swinging

...hard

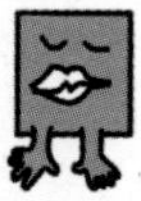

Can you write a poem where you get knocked down but get up again?

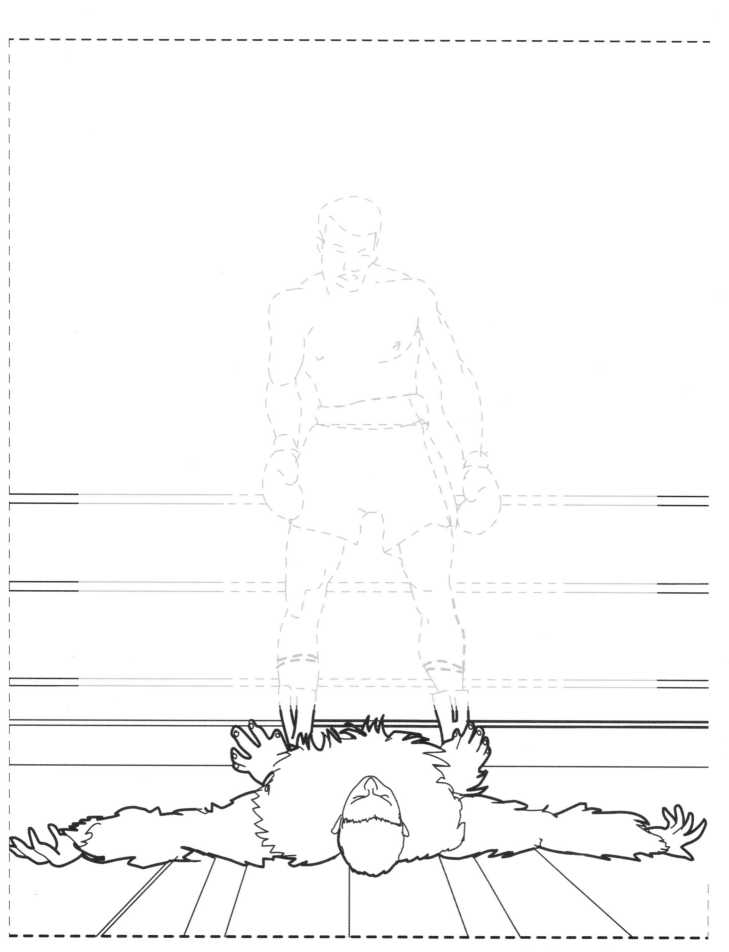

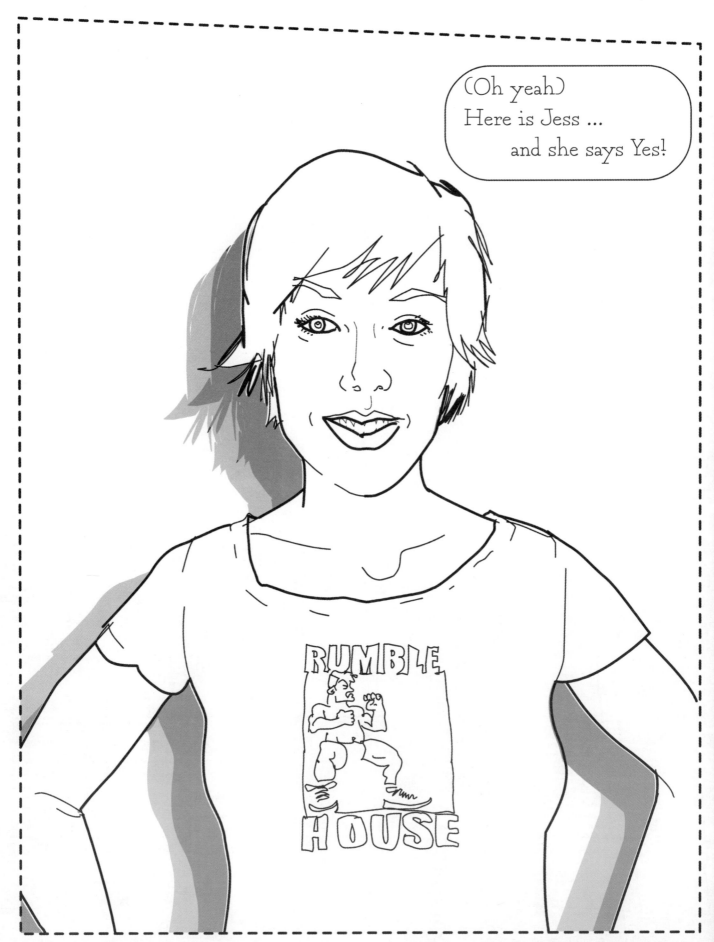

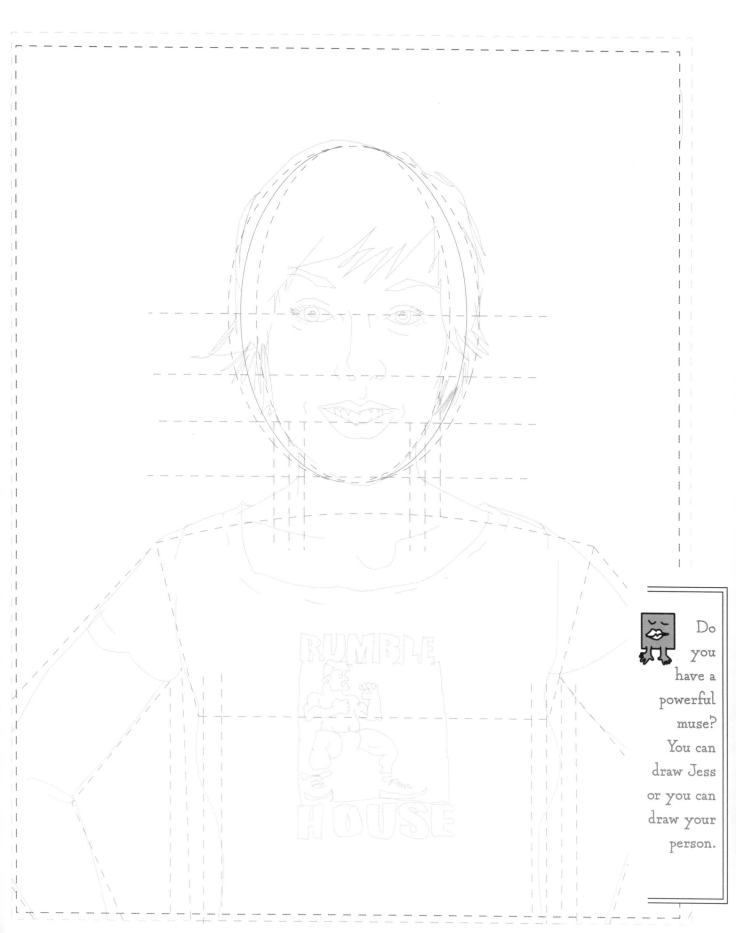

Do you have a powerful muse? You can draw Jess or you can draw your person.

We take down the sign. We talk about starting over.
But not as Gorilla House.

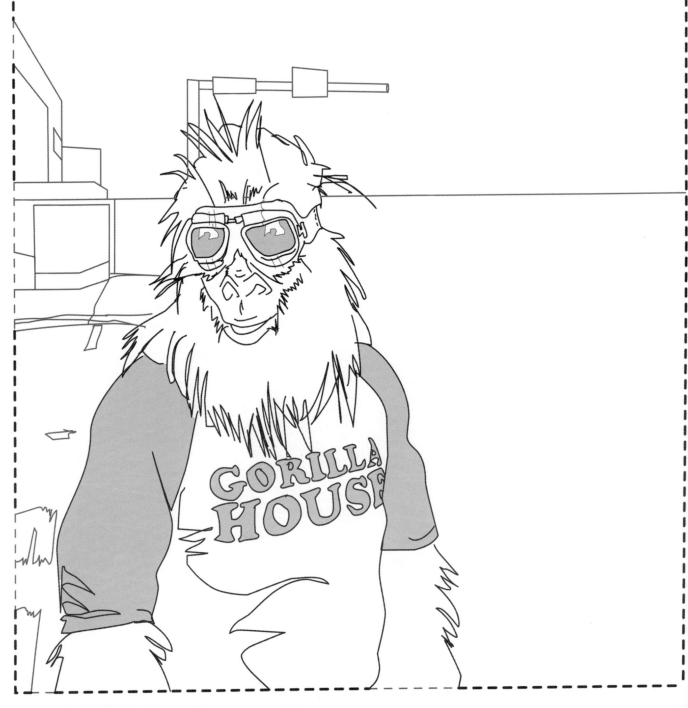

People ask, "Why would you give up your brand recognition?" Some of them get quite angry. My response is that Gorilla House has its own character in this story. The building is part of the tribe. When your dog dies, you can get another one, but you probably won't name it

SKIPPY PART II.

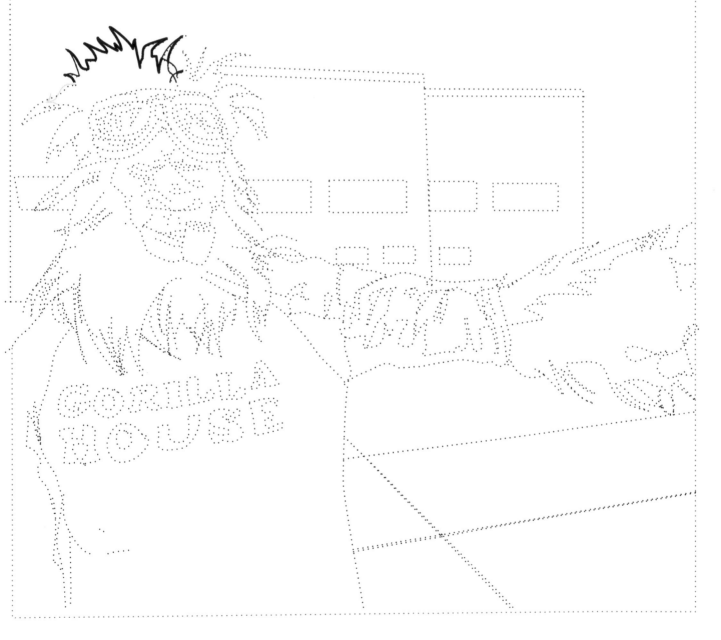

Get up man

(talk myself out of bed)

Get up son

(I'm tired I'm fed up)

Get up fool

(No more, please no more)

Truth?

(Truth)

Truth is you aren't smart

enough to rest... ever

and you're lucky

and you're strong

so get out of bed or

you're going to get rolled over

by a world built for squares

(I hate you so much)

You my friend, are a rhombus

(I hate you)

...a wild beautiful rhombus

Can you write a poem where you celebrate a math shape? Trapezoid? Cone?

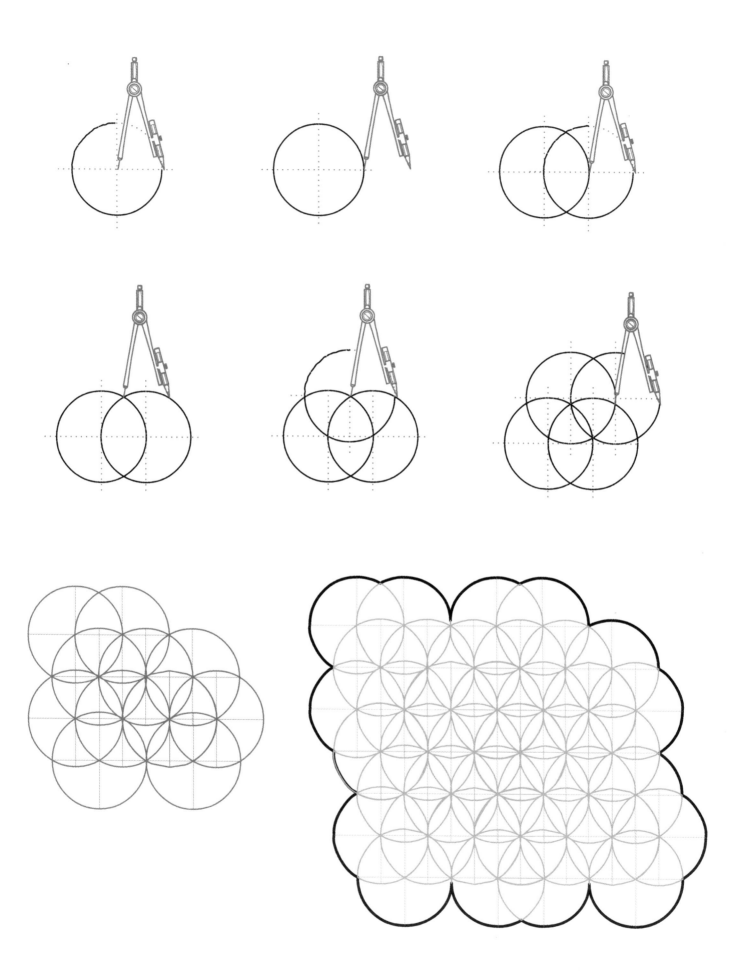

This guy named Kam shows up, and says point blank, "You can't close this place." As much as I appreciate the support, I try to explain it is impossible to pick up what we built and move it somewhere else.

We have a ton of empty offers to move our Gorilla House into other people's places. It's tiring to explain why moving locations won't work.

Kam persists and of all the people pushing me to start over, Kam gently asks if I'll go with him to see a space he found. I agree just as an excuse to get away from the vultures.

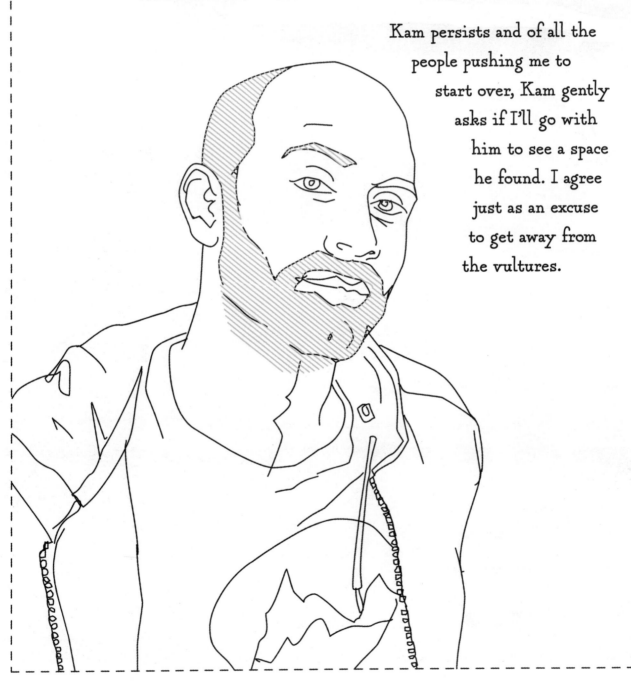

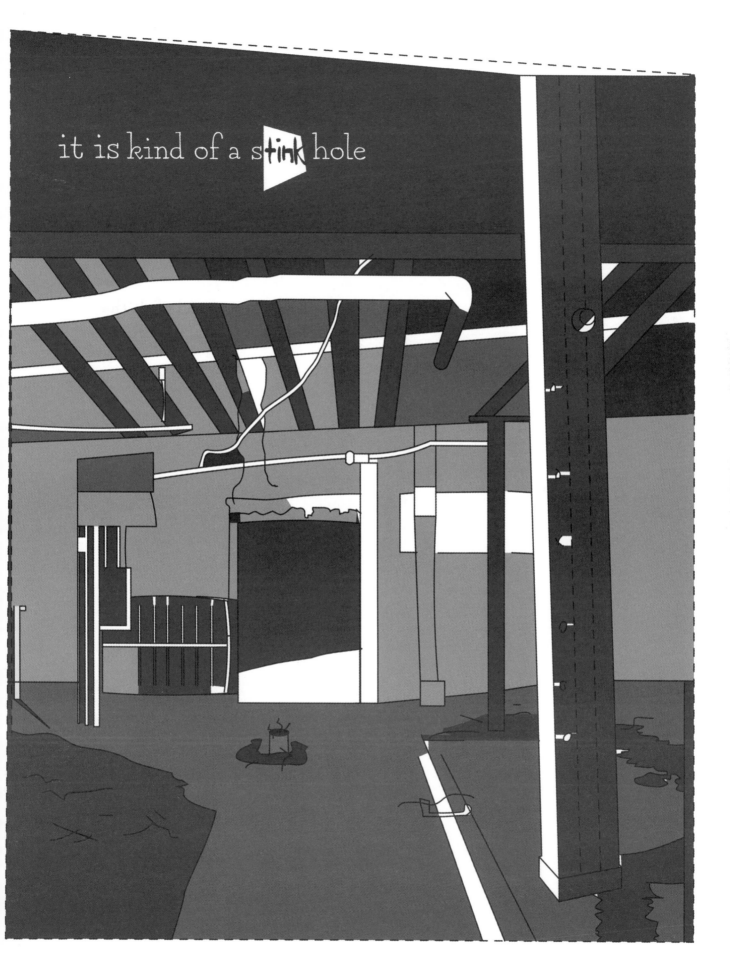

We spend six months working on a space that no one really knows about. We try writing plans for a Gentrification Project where instead of moving in, cleaning up and getting kicked out, we take over unliveable spaces, infuse love, hard work and passion, bring the space back to life and eventually move out to the next location.

In the six months after losing Gorilla House, we work for 150 desperate days trying to pull our second gallery together. No matter what we try, we just can't do it.

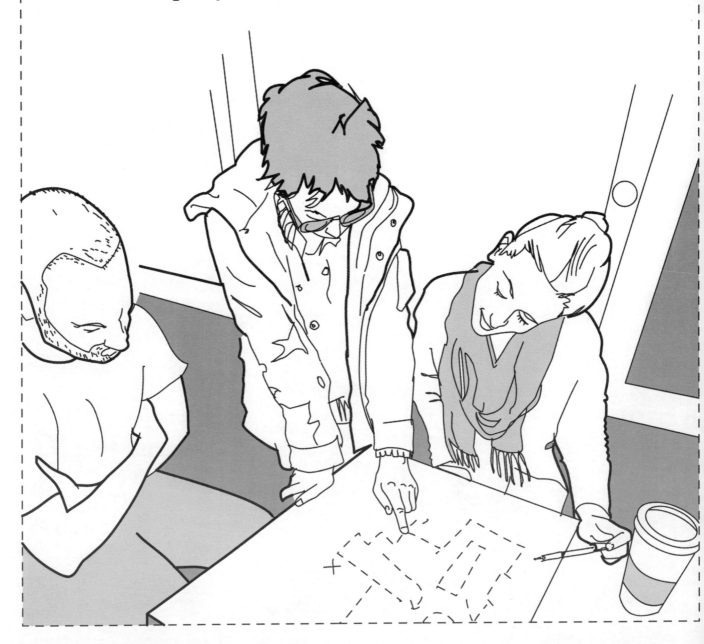

We pack it all up, buy a van and drive to California.

Despite all my confidence that we are loved, I'm not even sure anyone
                will miss us.

Did
you
ever
have to
overcome
the
feeling
that
no
one
cares?

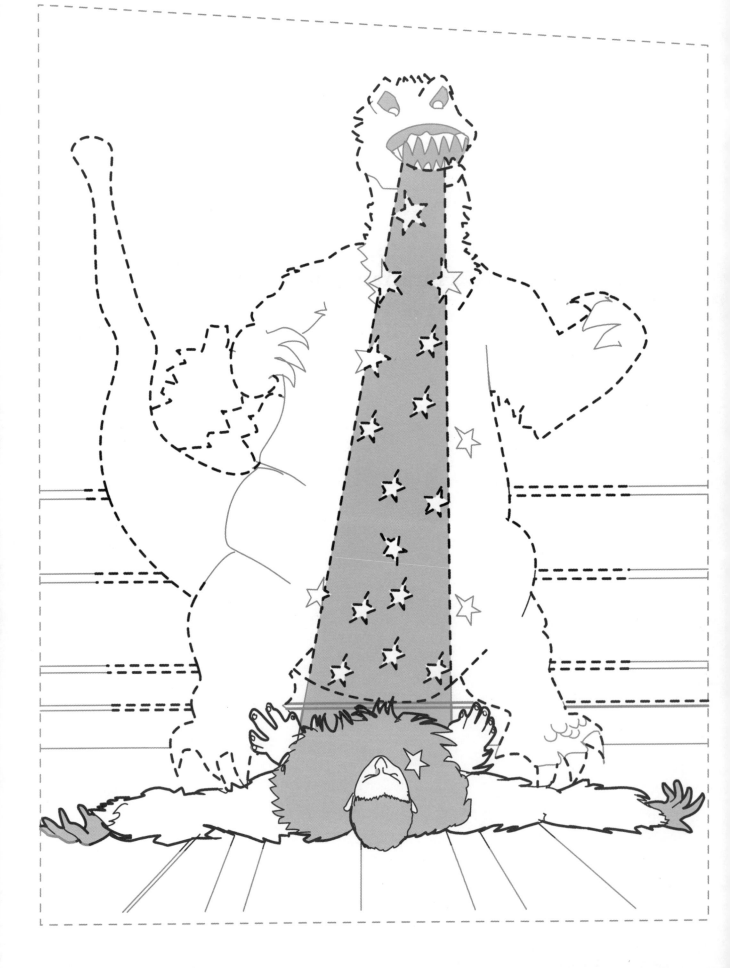

Abraham and Alexander

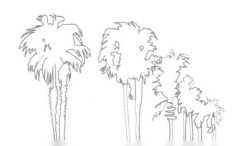

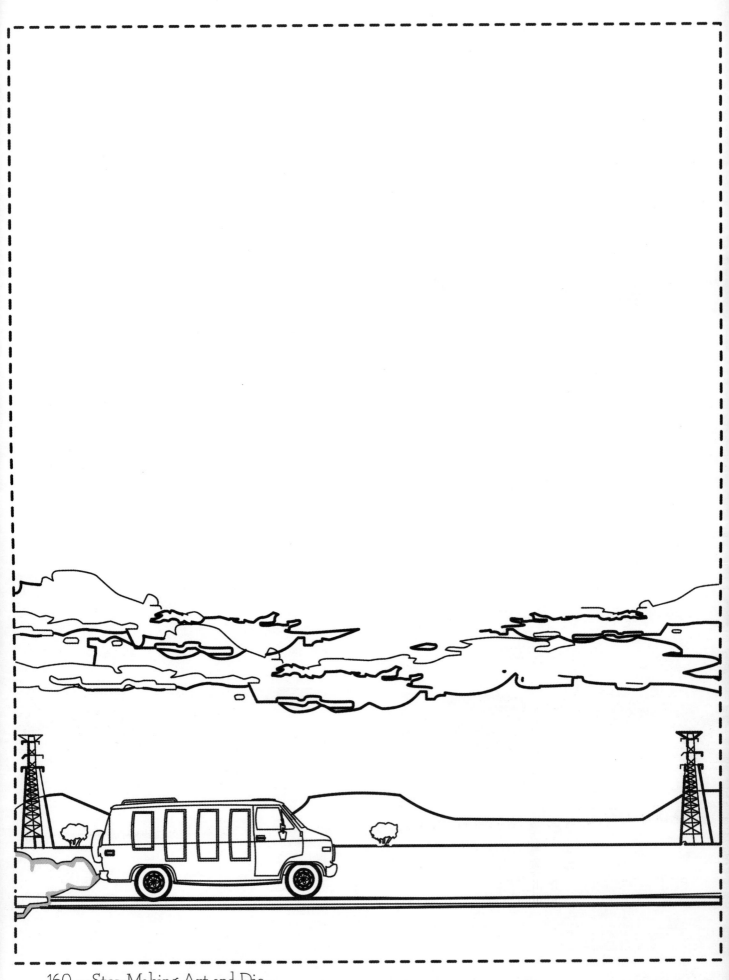

From home, we drive five blocks east, turn left on the main road, which becomes the main highway, which becomes the huge freeway, which terminates in Santa Monica, California. It takes four days.

Our spot #171 on Venice Beach is 2,500 kilometers down the street from our apartment.

Ape's out of his cage,
man ape is out of his cage.

*spot # 171

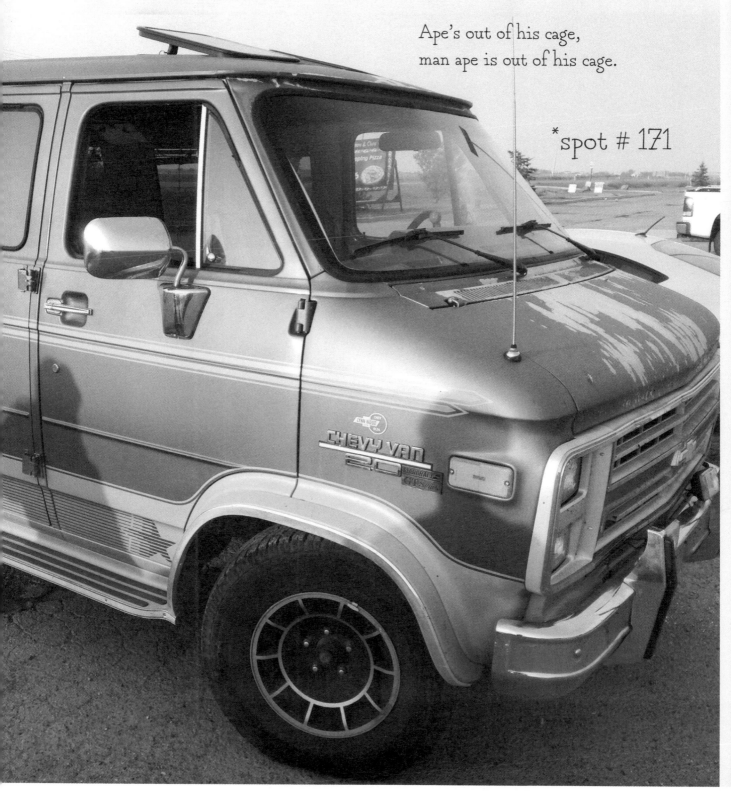

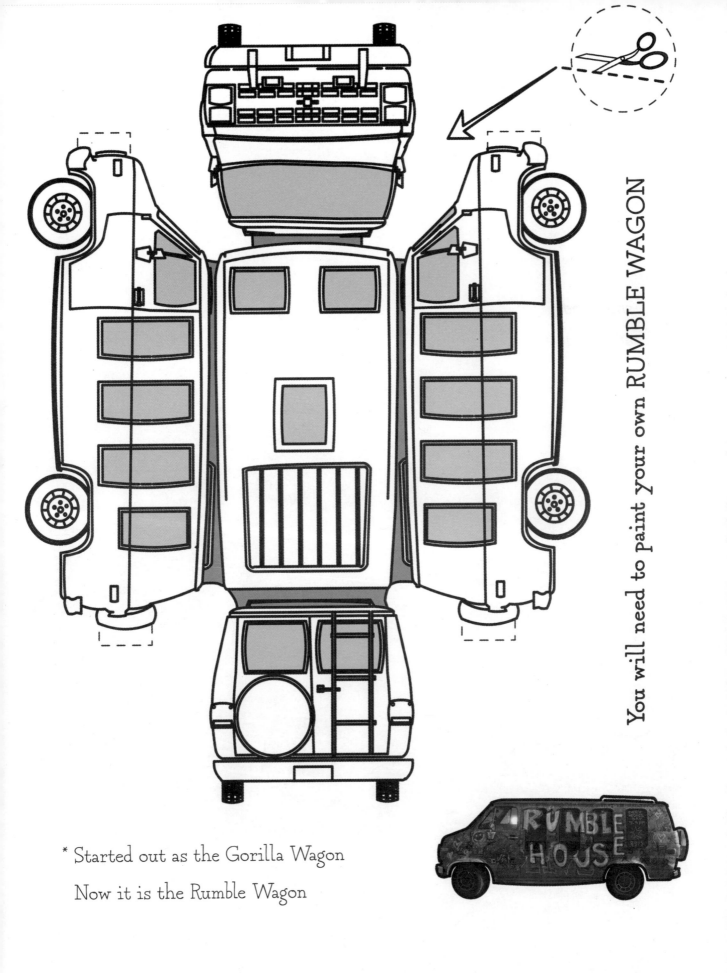

You will need to paint your own RUMBLE WAGON

* Started out as the Gorilla Wagon

Now it is the Rumble Wagon

when the

sky is dim

and everything

has gone awry

and my eyes

too blunt

to see

she stands

at my side and

oh god she is so

radiant she burns

my sorry eyes

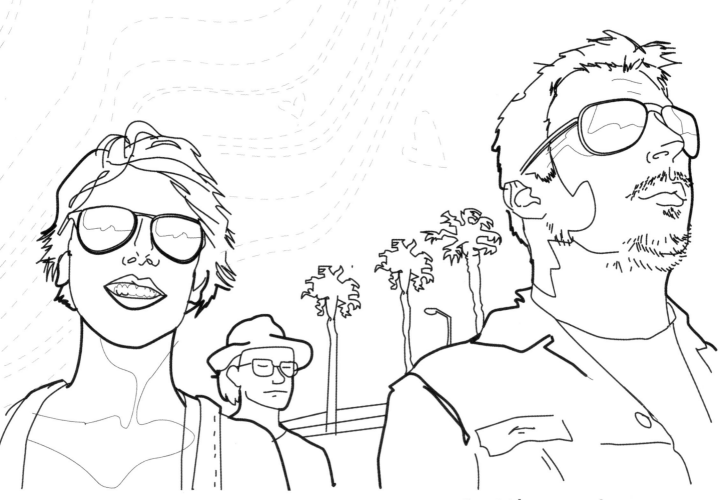

When you get to Venice Beach, find the old gnarly street prophet, Abraham (Ibrahim). Don't pester him if he's busy, but if he looks at you and smiles his toothless grin, go tell him your name. He will visit you with sage knowledge.

I buy Abraham a guitar, not out of obligation but out of respect. And every day for 14 days he stays next to me and keeps me and my family safe.

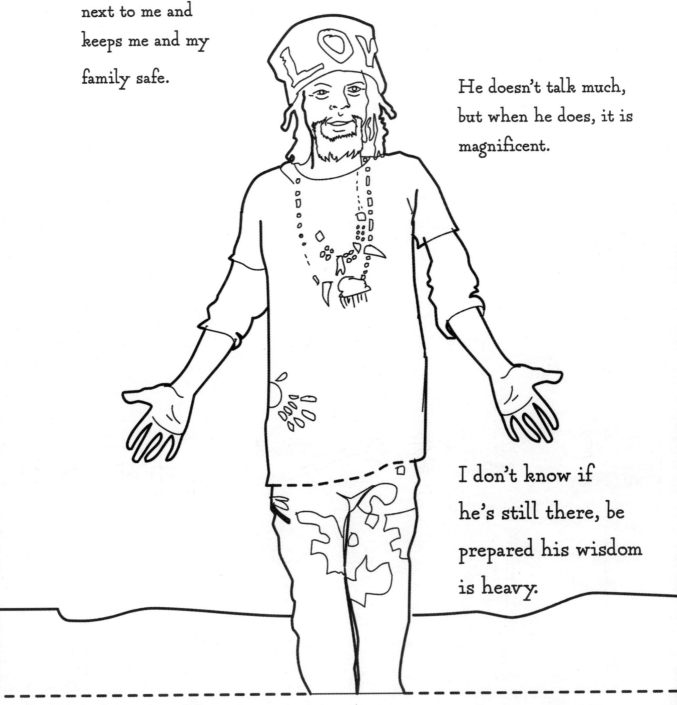

He doesn't talk much, but when he does, it is magnificent.

I don't know if he's still there, be prepared his wisdom is heavy.

For twelve hot days we set up a tent on Venice Beach, and paint forty paintings. We trade forty paintings for forty good deeds.

We trade one painting with a dentist who flies home to Atlanta and gives away a free dental extraction to someone without insurance.

One painting goes to a man named SHARKOS who returns to prison to read books to other prisoners.

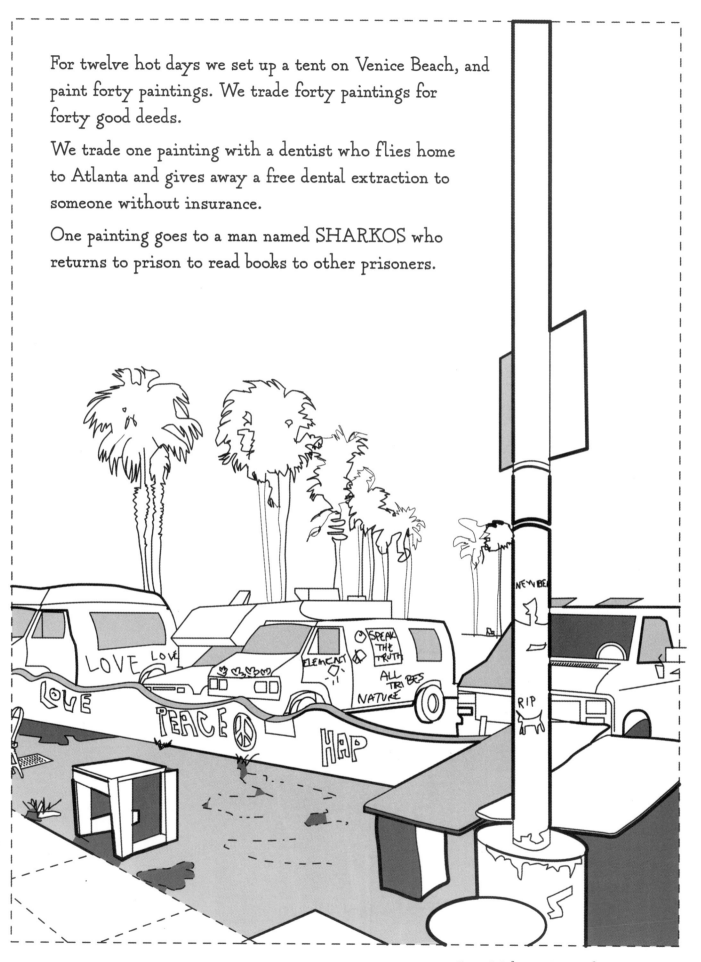

When you paint plein air painting (outside) what you really want to capture is the radiance and the colour of things. Sometimes I go out to mix colours.
Chase those things you can't take home in your sketches and photos.

RED MUD SLOPE
_ _ _ _ _ _
_ _ _ _ _ _

☐ _ _ _ _

☐ _ _ _ _ SPECTRUM RED

☑ VIOLET
_ _ _ _

☑ NAPLES YELLOW
_ _ _ _

darkest of leaves		

_ _ _ _ _ _
_ _ _ _ _ _

☐ _ _ _ _
☐ _ _ _ _

☐
☐

lightest of leaves

_ _ _ _ _ _
_ _ _ _ _ _

☐ _ _ _ _
☐ _ _ _ _

☐
☐

sky dark blue

_ _ _ _ _ _
_ _ _ _ _ _

☐
☐ _ _ _ _

☐
☐ _ _ _ _

sky at lightest

_ _ _ _ _ _
_ _ _ _ _ _

☐
☐ _ _ _ _

☐
☐ _ _ _ _

dark grass

_ _ _ _ _ _
_ _ _ _ _ _

☐
☐ _ _ _ _

☐
☐ _ _ _ _

light grass

_ _ _ _ _ _
_ _ _ _ _ _

☐ _ _ _ _
☐ _ _ _ _

☐
☐ _ _ _ _

river peaks

_ _ _ _ _ _
_ _ _ _ _ _

☐ _ _ _ _
☐ _ _ _ _

☐
☐

green blue water

_ _ _ _ _ _
_ _ _ _ _ _

☐ _ _ _ _
☐ _ _ _ _

☐
☐ _ _ _ _

deep blue water

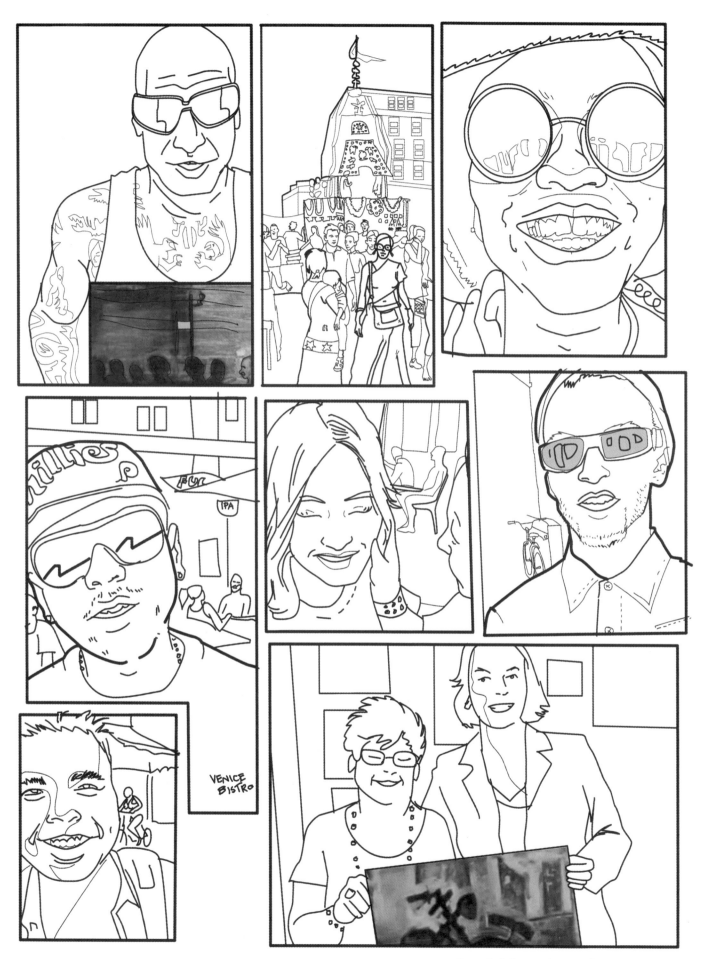

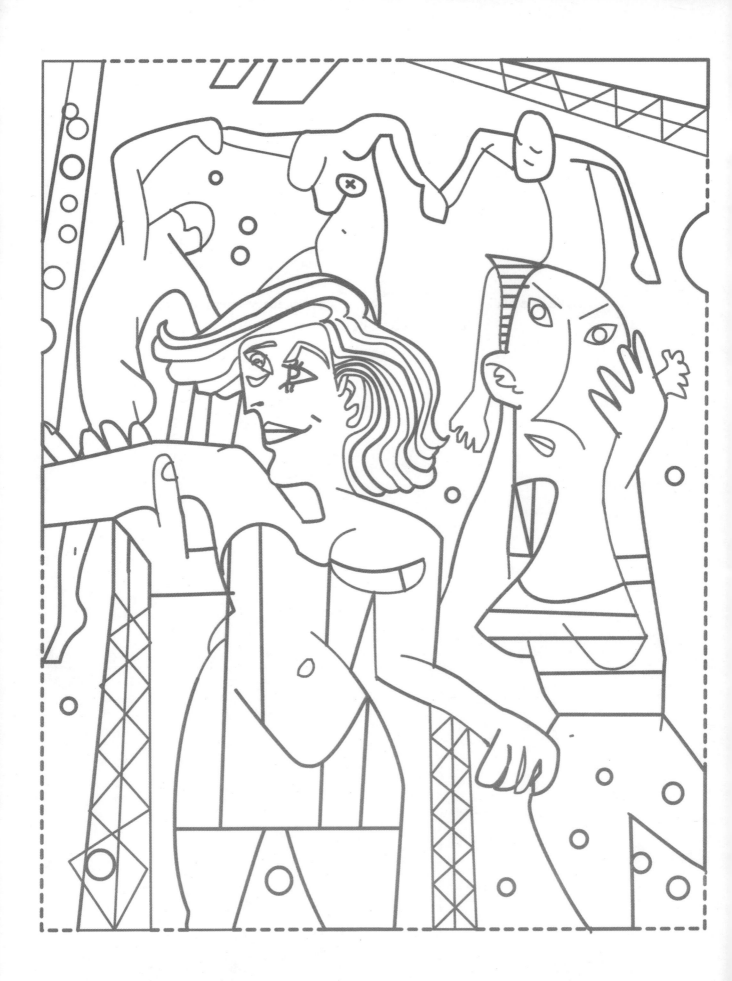

Abraham asks if we can have breakfast with his dear friend Alex.
He tells us that Alex is an artist and a writer, and that he knew
Picasso, Matisse, and Salvador Dali.

When we meet him it is magic.
After breakfast, he takes us to his house. It is filled with treasures.

He tells us about meeting Picasso when he was young.
We talk about art, he   tells us a lot about his wife.

We are all   completely carried away.

When we get   back to the beach, I look
up a photo of   him as a young man and
paint him.   I blast it out in about
twelve   minutes.
I want to   give it to him.

Jess   goes for art
supplies   and just as
I finish   she shows
up, and   asks, "is
          that
          Alex?"

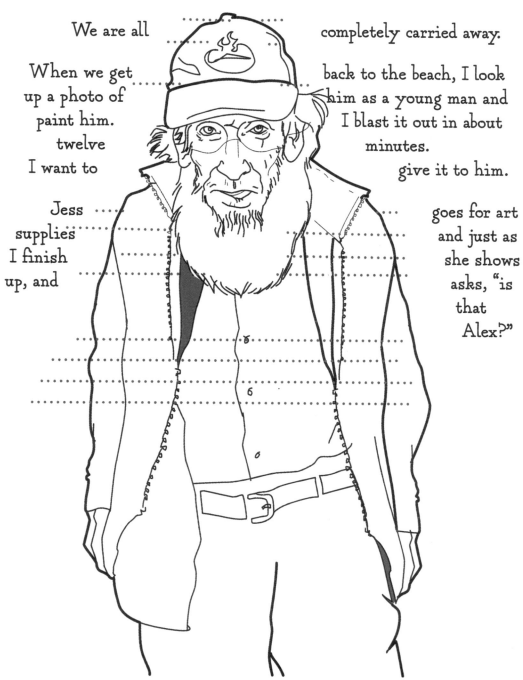

Alexander Eliot had been a world class art critic for TIME magazine. He'd lived among the masters and for some dumb reason, my thinking was that it would be okay to gift him with the painting I'd done of him.

We were leaving for home the next day and were supposed to meet meet him for breakfast before our departure.

Jess comes back from somewhere and started painting, but didn't say anything about his portrait. Finally I asked, "What did he say?"

"He didn't say anything," Jess said, "his gate was locked, so I chucked the painting over the fence."

At least I couldn't be disappointed. If he said he didn't like it, I probably would have given up painting forever.

The next day at breakfast was excruciating because he didn't say a word about it. I was embarrassed but finally I whispered to him, "Did you like my painting?"

He had no idea what I am talking about. He hadn't seen it.

Now this really is the perfect ending. I gave him the work and we had a chance to have breakfast and I never had to worry whether he thought it was any good.

I went home to the van, happy and content, and we say our good-byes forever.

A couple of hours later, Abraham walked over to me in my tent and whispered, "Hey Rich, look over there…"

Slowly I looked out and at about ten steps a minute, Alex shuffles towards us. Each day he walked a kilometer to the restaurant and back. Today he'd walked to the restaurant and home and then twice as far again to where we were set up on the beach.

He brought us his book SIGHT AND INSIGHT, 1959. Inside he wrote, "To Rich and Jess, Love Alex" and whispered, "You've renewed my hope."

There were lots of tears. We only knew this man for two breakfasts but saying goodbye to him was like losing a limb.

He was pleased by us and what we were doing. Again, my stupid mouth said, "Did you like the painting?"

He gave a shocked look, "I nearly died getting here." Which wasn't exactly to say he did or didn't like it.

But then he hugged me and leaned in to my ear to say, very quietly, something just for me to hear...

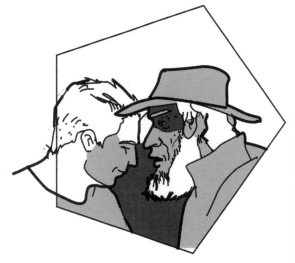

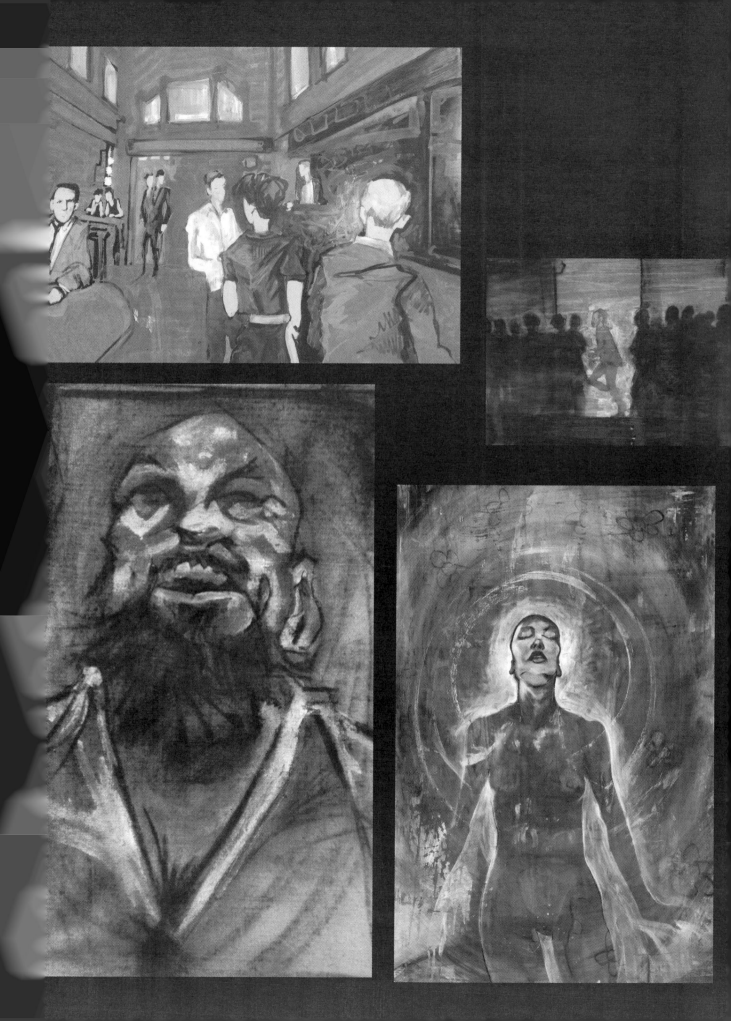

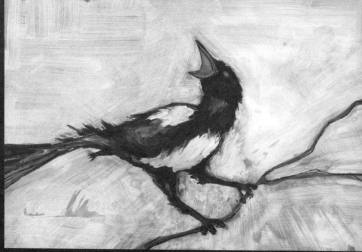

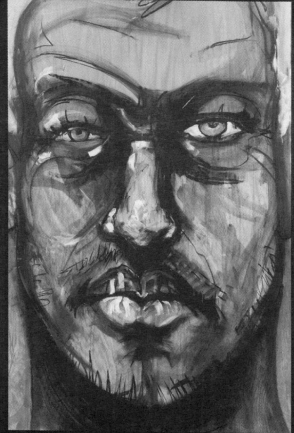

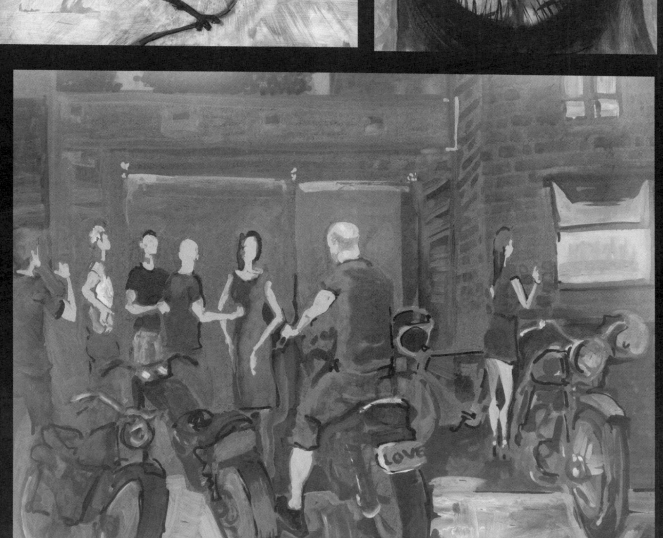

And then we write and embroider our Inclusionism Manifesto

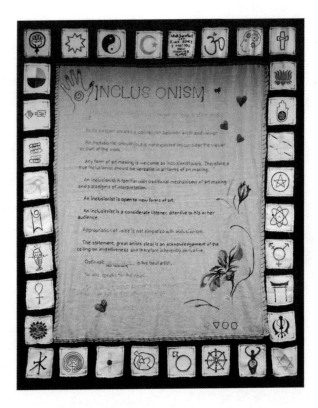

1) The moment of making art supersedes the residue of the work itself.
2) At its best, art creates a connection between artist and viewer.
3) A inclusionist should (but is not expected to) consider the viewer as part of the work.
4) Any form of art making is welcome as inclusionist work. Therefore a true inclusionist should be versatile in all forms of art making.
5) An inclusionist is familiar with traditional mechanisms of art making and paradigms of interpretation.
6) An inclusionist is open to new forms of art.
7) An inclusionist is a considerate listener, attentive to his or her audience.
8) Appropriation of voice is not simpatico with inclusionism.
9) The statement, "great artists steal" is an acknowledgement of the ceiling on inventiveness and therefore inherently derivative.
10) (your name here) is the best artist - you just became Inclusionist Leader Supreme.
11) No one speaks for the dead.
12) Once you accept your work is priceless, everything else is chump change.
13) Inclusionist means being vulnerable, when in doubt consult Kipling's: If.
14) Build something so true that even the people who would normally try and tear you down hold off to see if you make it.

(Be the River)

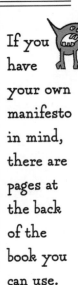

If you have your own manifesto in mind, there are pages at the back of the book you can use.

SURVIVAL ACTIVITY XIII

Discover the

thing

unseen

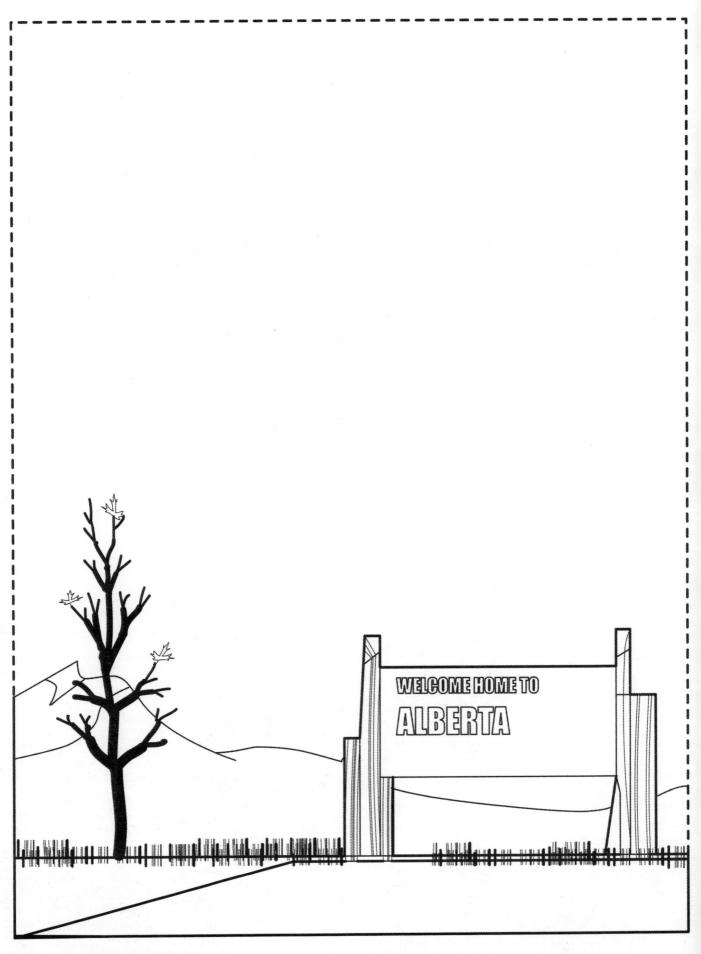

We come home. And without a place to paint again I sit and sulk. TEDx calls. They wanted to know if I wanted to **paint** at a TEDx event and I am truly sorry, but the lovely lady on the phone gets an earful.

To her credit, instead of being offended, or even hanging up ...

she just listens. Then she calls back and asks me to **talk**.

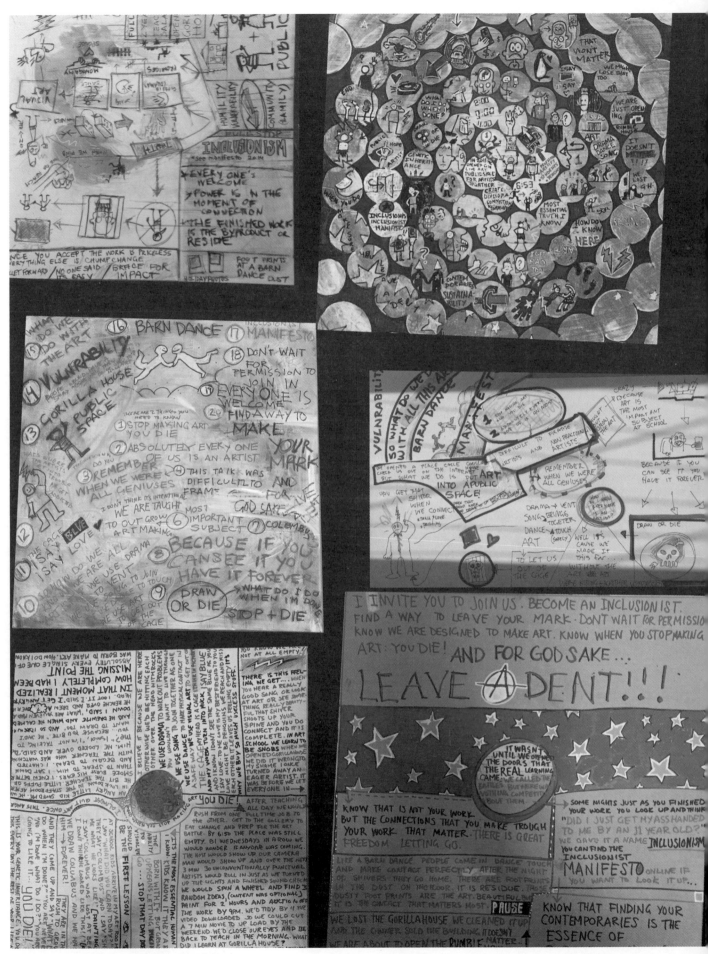

178 – Stop Making Art and Die

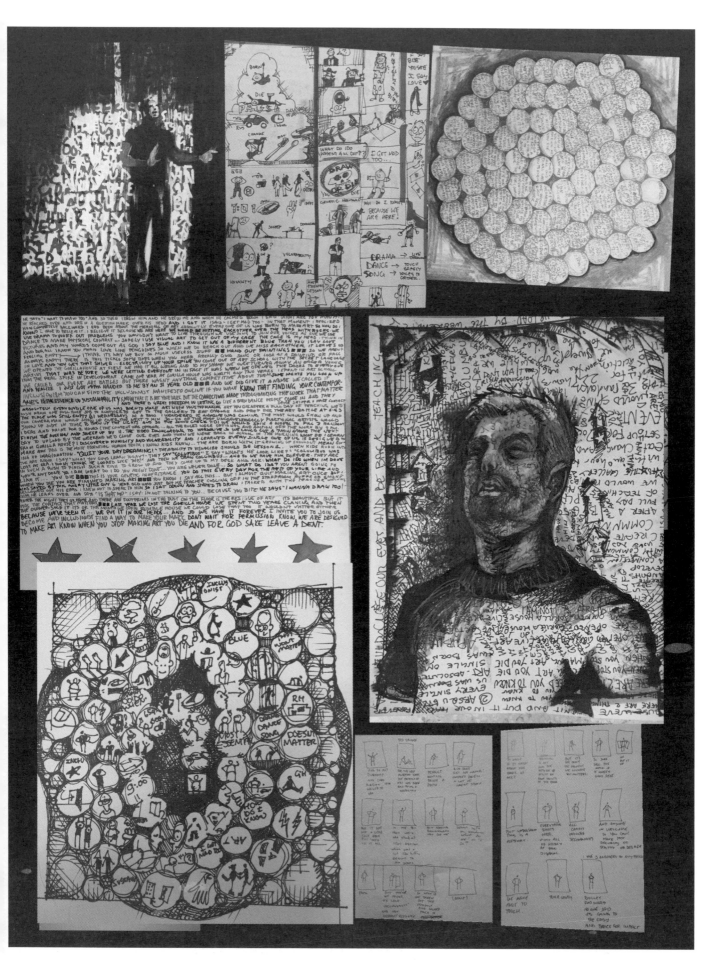

Stop Making Art and Die – 179

Preparing the TEDx talk almost kills me. I have five weeks to prepare and I rewrite my talk 67 times. Then I practice it over a thousand times before I get it right.

I have to invent my own way to study with my monkey brain.

I draw pictures of my talk over and over again, in bubbles radiating out from the middle.

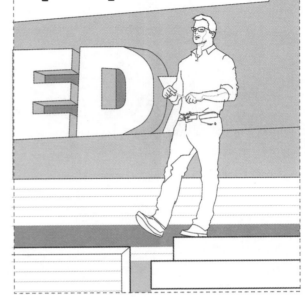

Absolutely every single one of us was born to make art. And when you stop making art, you die. In 2012, we opened the Gorilla House. It was a space for artists to gather, to make artwork in the public, and to connect with people. Every Wednesday - 81 Wednesdays in a row - we would rush down to the gallery after a full day of teaching, with an hour to set up, eat, change, and get ready for our seven o'clock event.

By 6:50, the place was empty. And I would wonder, "What am I going to do with this space?")

All at once, our host would arrive, our videographer would arrive, and about 30 or 40 professional artists, students, teachers and art instructors would all show up - just in time for sound check. We'd spin a wheel, come up with three random ideas - you could ignore the ideas if you wanted - and we'd paint for two hours with the public wandering in, bumping into us, talking to us. We auctioned the work off at nine [o'clock]; the auction is very special because the people in the auction saw the artwork being made.

By eleven o'clock, we'd be cleaning up and waiting for our video to download - we'd cut a seven-minute film to upload every weekend - and we'd get home just in time to close our eyes, to be back at school teaching the next day.

What did I learn at Gorilla House? I learned vulnerability...and humility. And I learned that every single one of us was born to make art.

Now, while kids know this, it needs to be the first lesson at school. So, I'd walk into the class-

room and I'd say, "What are you studying?"
[motioning to a painting]
This is by Carl White, by the way, one of my favourite painters

And they'd say, "Columbus!" And I'd say, "What does he look like?" So we'd look him up in a book, and I'd say, "No. Columbus was lost at sea. He didn't look like that." And so we'd draw him.
[Rich pointing to the drawing of Columbus; laughter from the crowd]
Can you see this in the back? That's pee.
[laughter from the crowd]
And for better or worse, he was in our heads - forever.
The kids were in a rush to finish; they'd come up to my desk and they'd say, "What do I do when I'm done?" and I'd say, "You're not done."
They'd say, "What do I do when I'm done?!" and I'd say, "You're not going to like it."
They'd say, "What do I do when I'm done?!" and I'd say, "You DIE."
[laughter from the crowd]
Then I explained to them: this is our genetic

heritage; you were born to do this. You're going to be reaching for this the rest of your life. And if you figure out what I have to say, you're going to draw every day until you're very old, and when you can't hold a pencil anymore, and you do die, then you can stop making art. But until then, you're not done.

I don't want to make it sound easy. I've quit many times. The last time, I'd just walked by the staffroom and there was this angry, little kid – he'd just bit his teacher. And I knew not to talk to him, so I sat down next to him, and started to draw, and he looked at me and he said, "Is that me?!" and I thought, I'm not talking to you, because you bite. [laughter from the crowd]

He said, "I wanna draw, TOO!"

I gave him a piece of paper, and I drew him and he drew me, and when he calmed down, I said, "What are you even mad at?" and he reached over and he put a question mark over top of his head. And I got it. And I said, "Yeah, man. Sometimes I get mad, too."

That's when I realized that I had art upside down, and that every single one of us was born to make art.

So, how do I know? Well, I know because we're here, and because otherwise we'd be smashing each other over the head with rocks. We use drama to solve problems that we wouldn't want to live through. We use dance to make a physical connection in a way that's safe. We use song to bring our voices together. I use visual art to get out of the cage; to me, the cage is my head. I say, I love blue... and I know I don't mean the same blue as you, and when I say "love", I mean I love you like my best friend, and you might be hearing, "He loves like...penguins!" and it leaves us feeling empty. And I think it's why we buy so much useless stuff.

It's not completely hopeless – because I think, every now and then, when you're reading Hemingway or you look at a Van Gogh, or you just look your best friend in the eye, you get this shiver that shoots up the back of your neck; you know you've made a connection. You know that it's real. It's why we fought so hard for our Gorilla House. We had battles and they weren't at all competitive. Every now and then you'd look at your painting like, I killed it... and then you'd look over and say, "I just got my ass handed to me by an 11 year old."

[laughter from the crowd]

It wasn't until we opened the doors to everyone we learned the magnitude of what we were doing. We gave it a name: we called "Inclusionism". We wrote the Inclusionist Manifesto.

To start, know that finding your contemporaries is absolutely essential to your sustainability. Know that making connection is everything. Know that there's great freedom in letting go of the art. If you can imagine walking into a barn dance – people are touching and moving, making contact; at the end of the night there's these dusty footprints on the floor. Those dusty footprints are the residue of the contact. They're evidence of what matters.

Our Gorilla House is residue. We've spent a year-and-a-half cleaning up our building and the owner sold the building, and for 11 months we had no house. Mmm...it doesn't matter. We've got a new space; it's called Rumble House — we could lose that, too. It won't matter, either. Because we've seen it – put it in our heads. We have it forever.

I would like to invite you to become inclusionists. Find your way to make your mark. Don't ask for permission. Know that every single one of us was born to make art, and that when you stop making art...

You die.

And when you do, make sure you leave a dent.

Thank you, very much.

-end transcription-

Transcript, Jennifer Théroux

> "You're going to draw every day until you're very old, and when you can't hold a pencil anymore, and you do die, then you can stop making art. But until then, you're not done."

No matter how hard you try or how much you give away....
nor how little you keep for yourself

"maybe if you'd listen to anyone zlery, we were all here for you, and I'm glad you lost it, you deserve it"

They said *you Andy* Warhol-ed them

I'm sorry, I don't think I know what that means

They said, you promised to make them famous and then took all the fame for yourself

WTF?

All you care about is yourself n you do no favours for real artists u steal joy n tramp on it. All the paintings u do of jess are horrible paintings if a beautiful women being blindsided by you its disgusting ur no friend to art or artists.. Paint or die u dont even know what that means

"I went to your dad's, gallery it's such a cool idea, too bad he's such a d`ick"

"hey I went to your teacher's art gallery it's such a cool idea, too bad he's such a `ick"

Your ego is consuming the community you are so desperate to create disappointed I watched your TED talk and I was disappointed

Pinko

Your ego is consuming the community you are so desperate to create

scab

I watched your TED talk and I was disappointed

ego

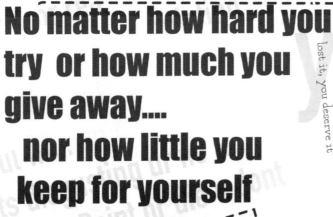

PEOPLE SAY REALLY NASTY STUFF

try hard

glad you failed

making it difficult for the real artists

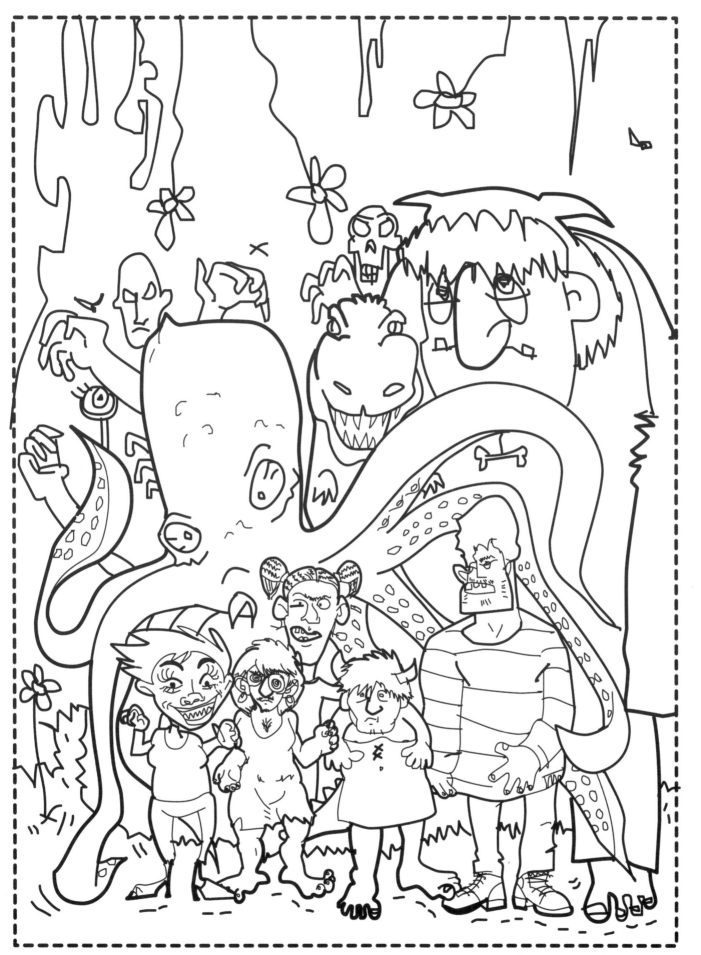

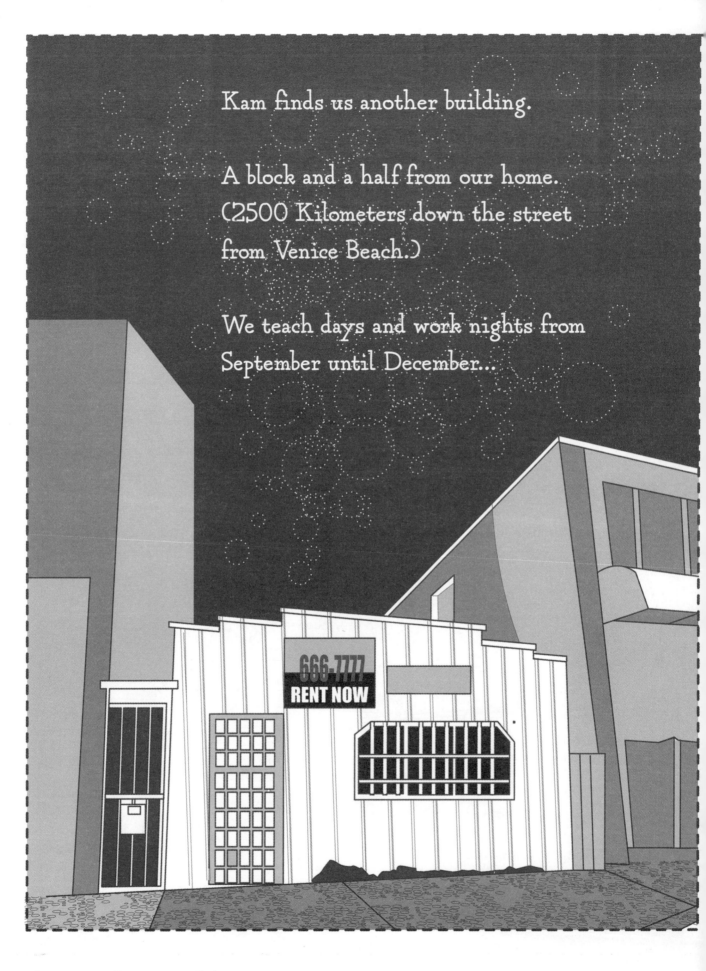

Kam finds us another building.

A block and a half from our home.
(2500 Kilometers down the street
from Venice Beach.)

We teach days and work nights from
September until December...

The new place is kind of a stinkhole too.

Generally if we can afford it for an art house, it's probably because no one else in their right mind wants it.

We don't want to keep cleaning up buildings to bring up our rent, only to be kicked out for our effort.

But we start over for the third time in under two years, undaunted.

And we decide on a shift of perspective.

Instead of cleaning up the joint and getting kicked out, we decide to treat ourselves like an urban gentrification project.

We find a new home, clean it up with the intention of walking away.

As in many cases intent is everything.

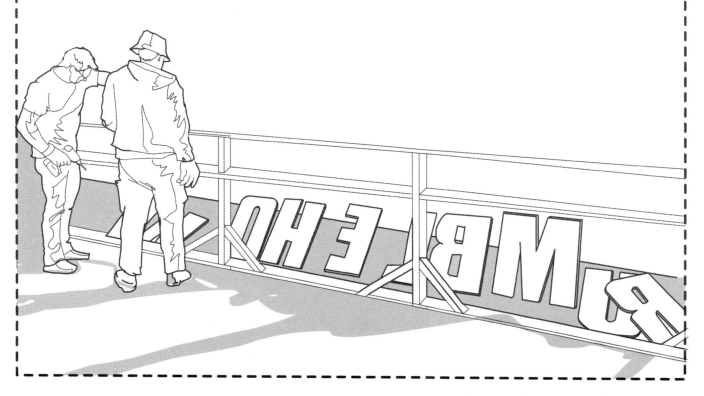

Feed the worst people

In your life gentleness

Kindness and love

Until they start to crave

It more than air

around them

If
you
dislike
someone
who
deserves
kindness,
write
them a
poem like
this.

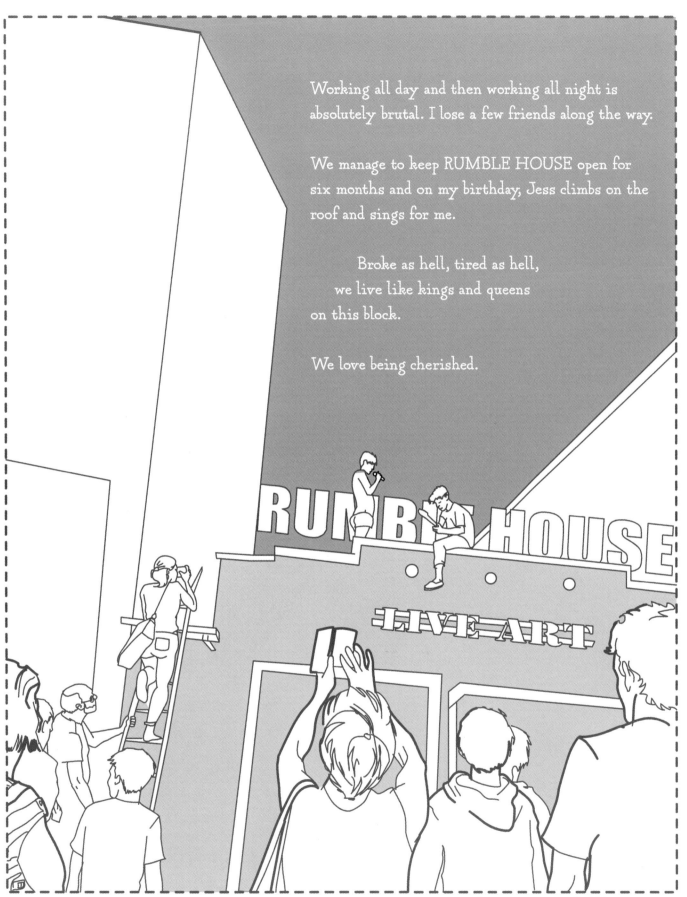

Working all day and then working all night is absolutely brutal. I lose a few friends along the way.

We manage to keep RUMBLE HOUSE open for six months and on my birthday, Jess climbs on the roof and sings for me.

Broke as hell, tired as hell, we live like kings and queens on this block.

We love being cherished.

Queens and Kings.

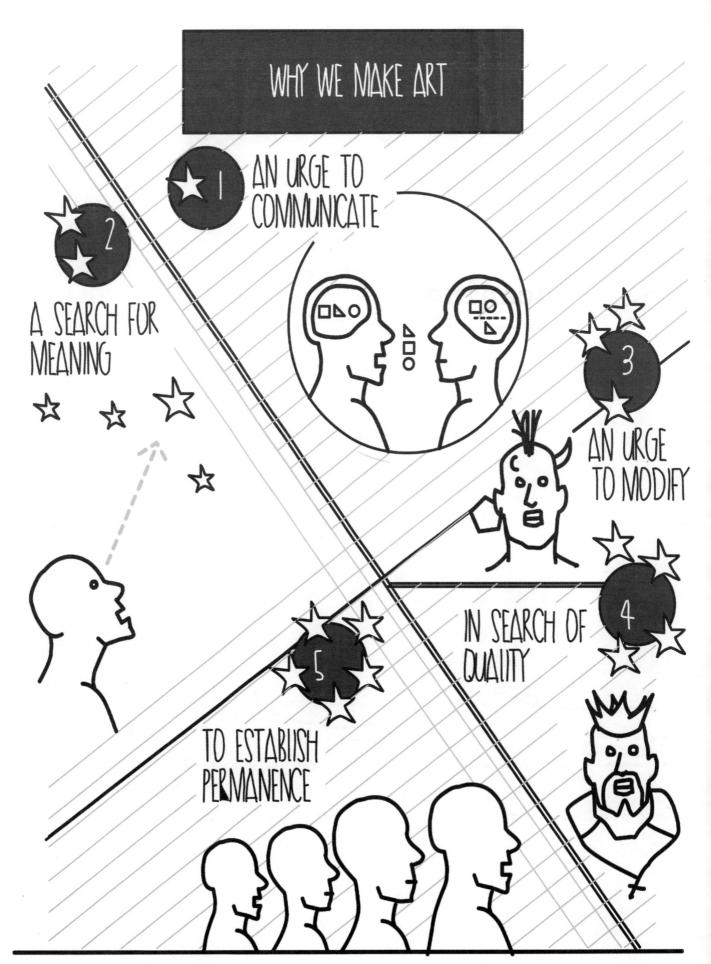

WHY WE MAKE ART

1 AN URGE TO COMMUNICATE

2 A SEARCH FOR MEANING

3 AN URGE TO MODIFY

4 IN SEARCH OF QUALITY

5 TO ESTABLISH PERMANENCE

Write down the name of the most beautiful thing you have ever seen. What give it such beauty or quality?

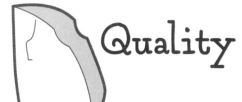

Quality

_____

_____

_____

_____

_____

_____

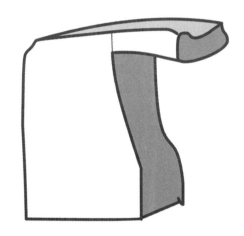

Meaning

Think of the most difficult idea you have ever tried to comprehend and draw it as best you can.

Modify

What is the thing you won't stop modifying (even though you know you should stop).

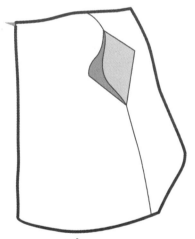

Permanence

Imagine an object you could leave on this green earth to be remembered forever.

Communicate

As best as you can, think of a thing you've struggled to communicate and draw a picture of it.

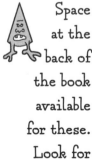

Space at the back of the book available for these. Look for the page called Code QMMPC.

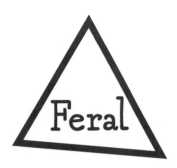

Are you still wild?
How can you stay wild?
What challenges do you face?

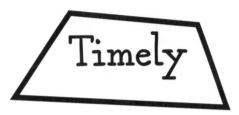

Are you ahead or behind the times?
What is the aspect of your work
that is timeless?

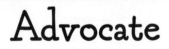

What can people really dig about
what you are doing?
All people? Some? Who then?

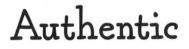

Who is your advocate?
How does this relationship
benefit you?
How does it benefit them?

Are you for real?
How do you know this?

Alex said that each great work of art had to be a thing that is seen and a thing unseen. Picasso said it was the space between the strokes that mattered. Hemingway spoke of the things left unsaid, while Buddy Rich said it was a space between the beats, and Miles Davis said it was a space between the notes. Henry James implied you must read between the lines.

Then maybe it is in the space between
that the thing unseen
slips through?

It's time for you to
go make a dent.

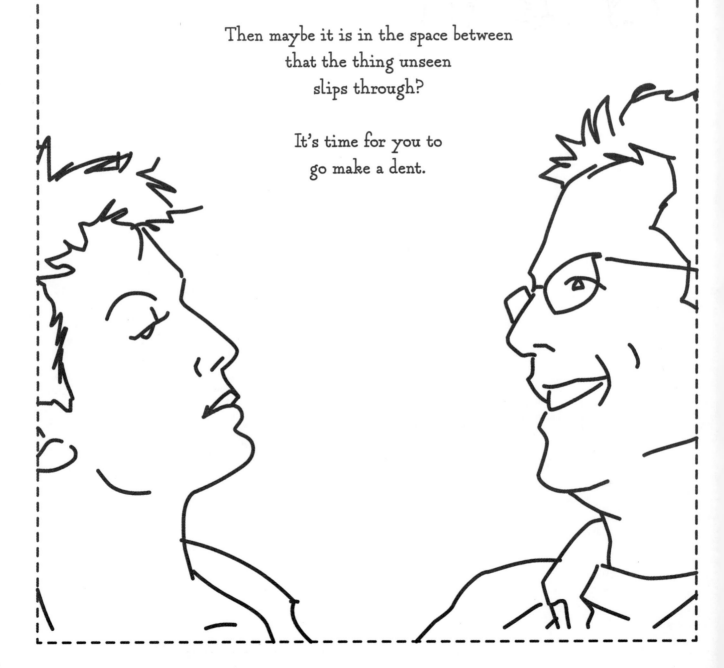

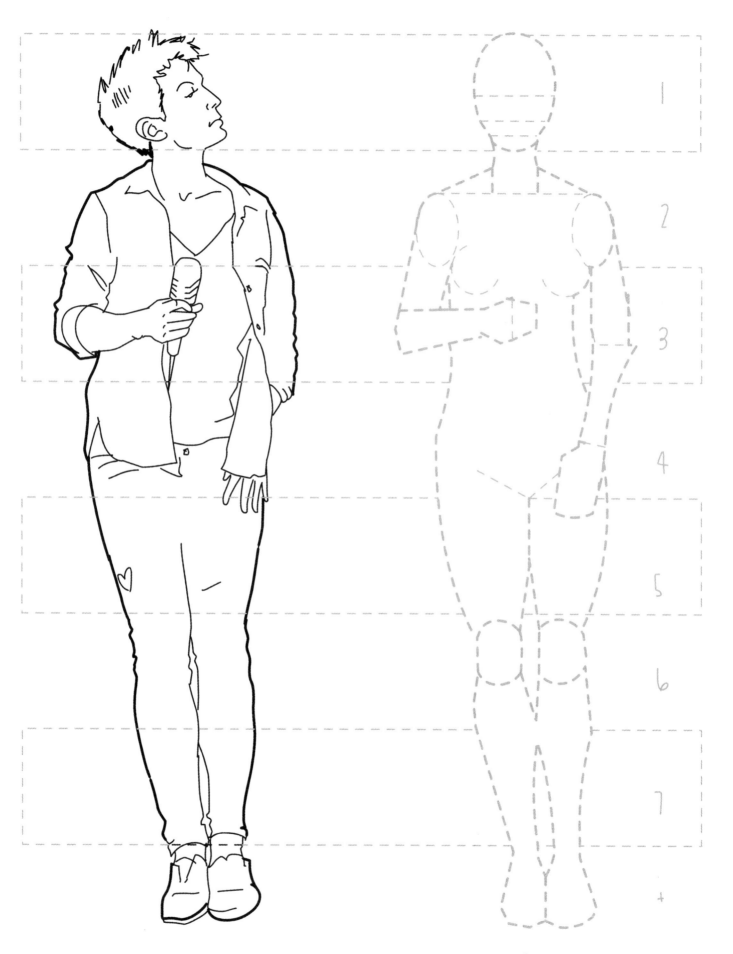

2

3

4

5

6

7

+

So many bodies

pass through

this door

eating

writing

painting

teaching

fighting

loving

taking

leaving

touching

the walls

touching us

I barely recognize

myself from the

fingerprints

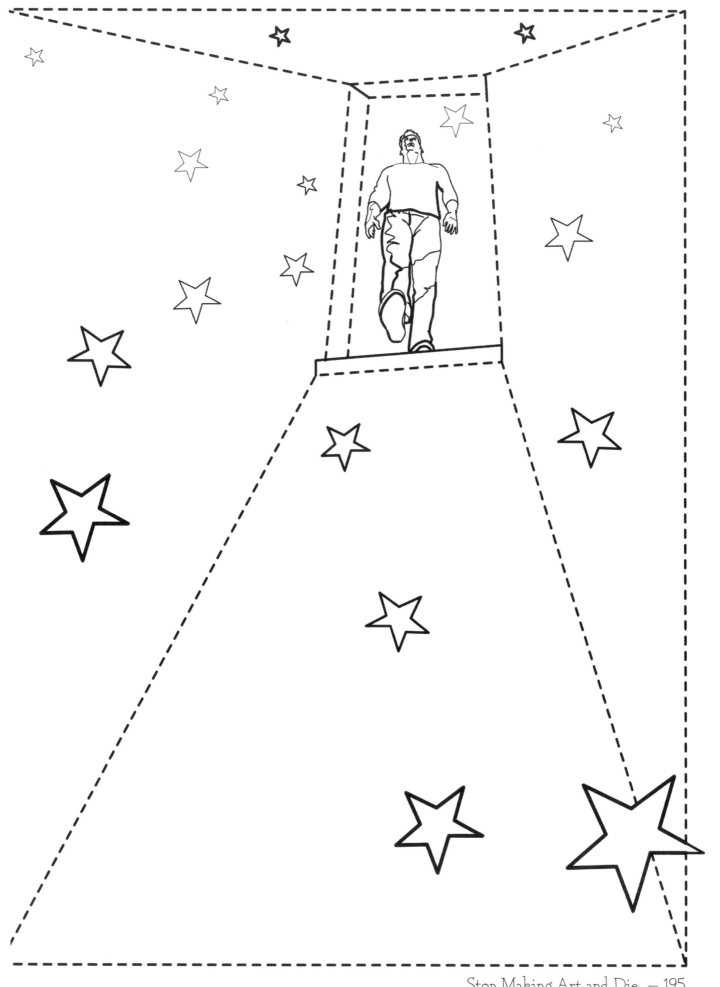

You might need a page to test out words that go together for poetry.
Or use for code **QMMPC.**

A PAGE FOR SURVIVOR ACTIVITIES

Here's a great sheet to scramble up your page 23
Things You are Madly in Love With, cut out, rearrange, find patterns.

A PAGE FOR SURVIVOR ACTIVITIES

This is the other side of the page you cut up. It's history.

A PAGE FOR SURVIVOR ACTIVITIES

You could paste the pieces here if you want.

 A PAGE FOR SURVIVOR ACTIVITIES

Draw in some of your favourite album covers.

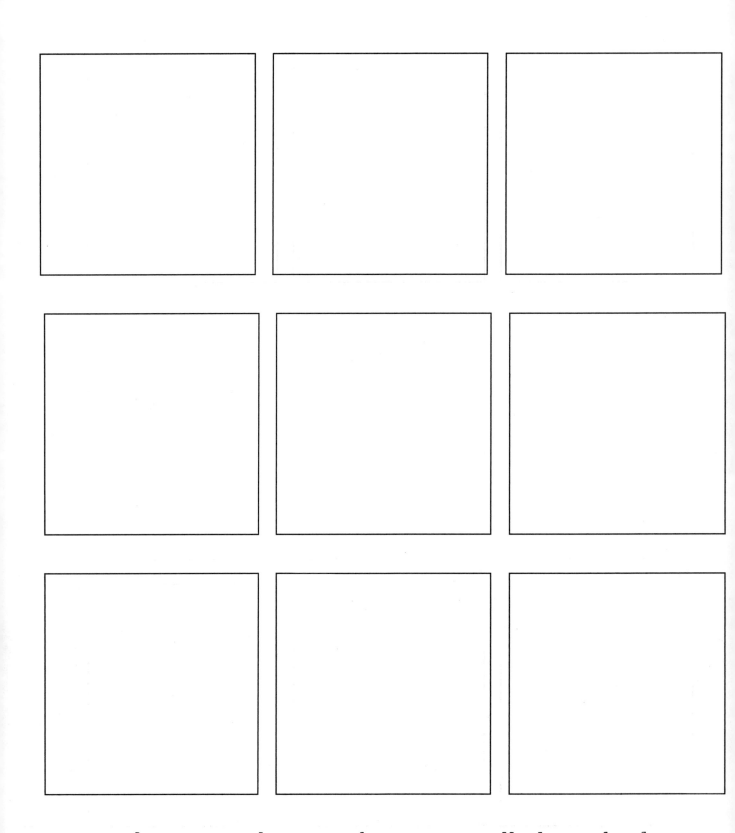

Make sure you listen to this music. Really listen hard.

A PAGE FOR SURVIVOR ACTIVITIES

Draw in some of your favourite books.

Read the words and the meanings between the lines!

 A PAGE FOR SURVIVOR ACTIVITIES

We didn't give you much of a chance to figure draw so take your clothes off, or some of them, check the mirror and draw yourself.

A PAGE FOR SURVIVOR ACTIVITIES

Friends or pets are fine to draw too. Or you can
write down their names like I have on the next page.

My early adopters, thanks to you all!

Aaren Szabo, Aaron McCullough (photographer), Aaron Navrady, Aaron Sidorenko, Abraham Butler, Adam Muzychuk, Adam Zhu, Akinna Kronemeyer, Alana Marchetto, Alexander Eliot, Alexander MacGillvray, Alexandra Chan, Amanda Ho, Amanda Siebert, Amyn O'Sulý, Andrea Rose, Andrea Ross, Andreas Tiedemann, Andrew Bolton, Andrew Sabo, Andrew Wedderburn, Andria MacDonald, Andy Szarka, Angela McCullough, Angelika Czabaj, Annie Coventry, Anyssa McKee, April Clay, Arne Fulton, Arvid Wangen, Asa Boufford, Astrid Deslandes, Audrey Redman, Austin Gallant, Banafsheh, Mohseni Khalesi, Belinda Fireman, Bill Bunn, Bill McNarland, Bing So, Bobby Whalen, Brandyn Storms, Bronwyn Schuster, Bruce Robertson, Bruce Watson, Calum Robertson, Cameron Davidson, Carla LaFramboise, Carly Marrs, Carmen Vazquez-MacKay, Cass Laurion, Cayley O'Neill, Centofanti Melisa, Chaleur Jones, Charlotte Beeger, Charlotte Daydreams, Chen Li, Chris Boyd, Chris Zimmel, Coby Schneider, Colin Smith, Connor Scott, Dani Christopher, Daniel Lindley, Darcy Bross, Darcy Lisecki, Dario Jajarmi, Dave Dai, Dave Hoare, David Ramsey, Dawn Desmarais, Dawn Escobar, Debbie Desmarais, Deborah Szabo, Dee Skappak, Delaney Lamont, Denby Royal, Dennis Tan, Derek Bøe, Des Pressey, Désirée Rose, Devin Hauswirth, Doug Nhung, Doug Wong, Dylan Tootoosis, Ed Drake, Edina Antoinette, Edric Escalante, Eileen Kosasih, Elena Bushan, Elena Evanoff, Elijah Escalante, Elizabeth Kinsman, Ellen Liguori, Emily Mitchell, Emma Grace May, Emre Cords, Enriquito Selfismo, Eric Willis, Erin Myers, Ethan Collister, Eugene Stickland, Eugenio J. Capistrano, Felix Theroux, Fernando Morales, Francis Willey, Frank Keller, Freya Gawdess, Freyja Ulveland, Fruitkake Forstner, Gareth Mack Howell, Gato Gallegos, Geoff Zimmel, Georgette Swenson, Ghaiss Hajj, Gisa Mayer, Good looking Daniel, Graham Fergie, Gwyn Auger, Halyna Skala, Harold John Pendergast, Hyla Stuijfzand, Ivan Eagletail, Jack Bride, Jack Morris, James Shurmer, James Tremain, Janice Marie, Janice Mather, Jaroslav Svoboda, Jaryd Adairski, Jayda Karsten, Jeff Watt, Jen Bee, Jen Stinson, Jennifer Park, Jennifer Theroux, Jeremy Salazar, Jeremy Simes, Jessica Szabo, Jessica Bruhn, Joanne Sparkes, Joel Monea, John F. Ross, Johnny Le, Jomar, Jon Sawyer, Jonny Vegas, Jordan Gioplasty, Josef Terek, Joshua Stanton, Julie Rubin, Kaie Jones, Kamil Lalji, Karen Klassen, Karen MacDonald, Kathleen Moors, Kayden Morrison, Kelly Isaak, Kelly Murphy, Ken Robinson, Kent Patel, Keone Friesen, Kevin Choo, Kevin Hayes, Khalil Alomar, Kimmi Luu, Kinga Bavinska, Koos de Jongh, Kyle Lovstrom, Kyle Messier, Lacy Dakota, Lane Shordee, Leigh-Ann Squire, Leslie Hill, Letmebe Frank, Leynes Sabatino, Linda Cunningham, Lisa Murphy Lamb, Lisa Nadeau, Lissa Christie-Cairns, Logan Cameron, Lonnie Desorcy, Lorene Shyba, Lori Stewart, Lorna James, Lorrie Matheson, Luella Gilchrist, Mahtab Nabian, Margot Baker, Marika Smythe, Mark Griffiths, Mark Hopkins, Mark R Northcott, Mark St Amant, Mark Vazquez-Mackay, Martin Cairns, Martin Sadlon, Matt Dewald, Matt Manastyrski, Mel Wolski, Michael Collett, Michael Cooper, Michael DeBolt, Michael Roik, Michelle Beddows, Michelle Stroo, Mohammed Al-Ibrahim, Morgan Worth, Nadine Charman, Nasty Bob, Nathan Pino, Neil Reid, Nick Austin, Nick Rooney, Nicole Feline, Nishant Pyasi, Nooreen Kurji-Asaria, Ola Birch, Oliver Sparkes, One Fox Faraday, Paddy Duddy, Peggy Adams, Penny Tryphonopoulos, Pete Gorman, Peter Barnett, Pierce Gray Tilton, Priscilla Theroux, Rachael Seupersad, Rae Hope Pantalleresco, Rahim Sajan, Rana Ahmadova, Rebecca Sulley, Rhean Murray, Richard Hehr, Rieley Quirico, Ringo Velasco, Rita Reddy, Rizwan Asaria, Rob Dodds, Robb Price, Robin Sparkes, Robyn Scrutton, Rory Allen, Rucastles, Ryan, Sabrina Pinksen, Sachie Ogawa, Sahib Gill, Sam Pink, Samantha Ray Malach Verlaan, Sameena Darr, Sandra Charge, Sandra Montgomery, Sandra Safire, Sanja Lukac, Sarah-jane Newman, Sarah-Joy Goode, Sarosh Rizvi, Scott Clark, Scott Korek, Scotty Logue, Sean Marchetto, Sergio Gayton, Shannon McClennan-Taylor, Shauna Pascoe, Shawn Grover, Sheila McDonald, Silas Kaufman, Spud, Steph Jane, Stephen Riether, Tahl, Tamara, Tami McDonald, Tandy Malmstrom, Tara Handyman, Teresa Léon, Thayre Angliss, Theresa Sparkes, Tick, Tomko Lamb, Travis Wilson, Ty Semaka, Tyler Macza, Tyler Wolfguy, Ursula de Vries, Vicki LM, Vince E. Varga (photographer), Violet Griffiths, Wabijoh Sabi, Warren Leonhardt, Wendy Lees, Will Rice, William Ingenthron, William Martin, Winslow Eliot, Yulia, Zach Lowe, Zachary Abbott, Zhen Huang, Zitin Lamba.

A Page of Gratitude

A Manifesto is your beliefs and what life means to you,
written down. Here it will be your Mean-afesto.

Lay your left hand flat, trace, and fill in with courage and fortitude. High five. You're already making a dent.

A PAGE FOR SURVIVOR ACTIVITIES

Lay your right hand flat, trace, and fill in with brightness.
High five again. Enter the world and discover the thing unseen.

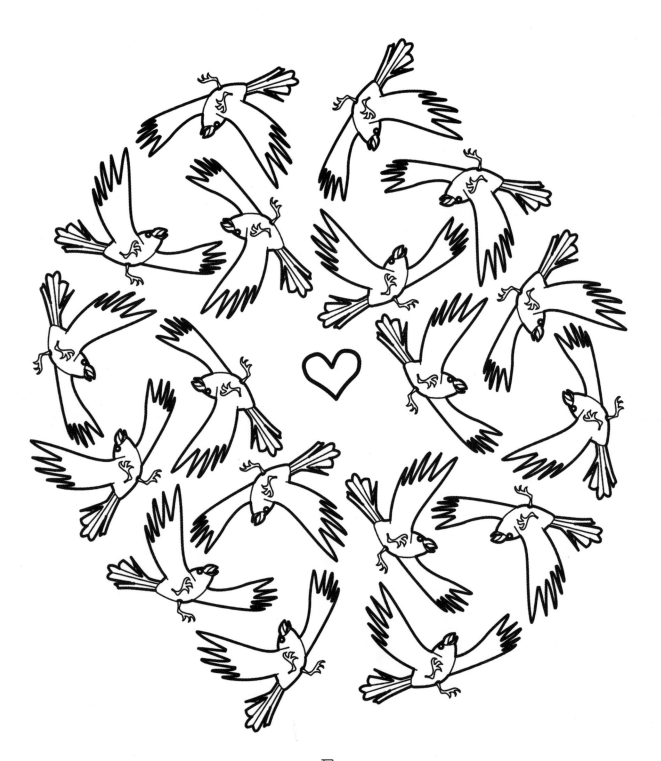

Fin